D0500029

RAPID
POPULATION
GROWTH

Consequences and Policy Implications

RAPID POPULATION GROWTH

Consequences and Policy Implications

VOLUME I
SUMMARY AND RECOMMENDATIONS

Prepared by a Study Committee
of the Office of the Foreign Secretary
National Academy of Sciences
with the support
of the Agency for International Development

Published for
the National Academy of Sciences by
The Johns Hopkins University Press, Baltimore and London

Published 1971 by The Johns Hopkins Press
Manufactured in the United States of America

The Johns Hopkins University Press, Baltimore, Maryland 21218
The Johns Hopkins University Press Ltd., London

ISBN 0-8018-1263-1 (clothbound edition)
ISBN 0-8018-1264-X (paperbound edition of volune I)
ISBN 0-8018-1427-8 (paperbound edition of volume II)

Originally published, 1971
Second printing, 1972

Johns Hopkins paperback edition, 1971
Second printing, 1972
Third printing (Vol. 1), 1973
Fourth printing (Vol. 1), 1975

Preface

In this book we attempt to define and describe the problems resulting from today's unprecedented rates of human population increase, and to help policymakers understand the implications of these problems. In its entirety the work contains a summary and recommendations (Volume I) and a collection of research papers (Volume II) by scholars representing several disciplines—economics, political science, sociology, demography, education, social ethics and public health. We hope that our conclusions will appeal to a wide audience, but we realize that many potential readers, especially busy and preoccupied government officials, are unlikely to have the time to study the more technical research papers upon which the policy recommendations are based. We have therefore decided that publication should take two forms: a clothbound edition containing both sections of the study, and a low-priced paperback edition of Volume I, the summary and recommendations. The paperback edition of Volume I is a self-contained unit and can be read as such; however, for the interested reader, references are made in the footnotes to the more detailed discussions in Volume II.

Early in 1967 the directors of seven U.S. centers for the study of population agreed that not enough is known about the economic and social effects of rapid population growth. This lack of knowledge has not, however, hindered the development of population policies and programs in a number of countries around the world. Some governments, seeing the specters of famine or of vast armies of unemployed, have moved forthrightly to help their people limit their own fertility. Other national administrations have stalwartly defended the need for more people to fill their empty lands or to provide the human engine for their march toward "national destiny."

Study and research about the physiology and chemistry of the human reproductive system proceed apace. Comparable research on the social and economic, political, and educational consequences of high and sometimes rising birth rates, falling mortality, differing age patterns in changing societies, and what a policymaker can do about these phenomena, has lagged sorely behind the research on demographic and contraceptive aspects of the problems. The center directors asked why this is so and whether something could be done about it. Dr. Roger Revelle, Director of the Harvard University Center for Population Studies, took the question to the then Administrator of the Agency for International Development, Mr. William S. Gaud, who in turn asked the National Academy of Sciences to design and execute this study. Dr. Frederick Seitz, President of the Academy at that time, appointed the undersigned as a special study committee, and requested Mr. W. Murray Todd, chief staff officer of the Office of the Foreign Secretary, to help in organizing and developing the study.

In the course of this work, two objectives have evolved: First, we have tried to understand some of the consequences (and to a lesser extent some of the determinants) of rapid population growth. We have limited ourselves to relatively short-term and clear-cut issues that are somewhat obvious, because these are the phenomena that concern the most people and about which policymakers must make decisions now.

Second, we have tried to separate some exceedingly complex problems into manageable components. In the past, much of the case for population limitation has rested on the presumed likelihood of exponential growth over rather long periods of time. Apocalyptic visions of the future are based on simple, mathematical extrapolation of present rates of population growth. We have asked a number of students of population to tell us what we really *do* know, on the basis of the carefully collected evidence, and what we *do not* know; their answers are reported in Volume II. From these papers and other evidence we have tried to derive a set of propositions about population growth and to infer some implications for the policymaker; these are contained in Volume I.

We have endeavored to examine the population problem as it affects us now—and for the next 5 to 30 years. The time dimension for any policy action that affects population is very likely to exceed the term of public office of the policymaker or planner. This means that the rationale for public policy on population must be so clear to the citizenry that the policy's life is not dependent upon the term of its political sponsor. Thus we try to make the case for public understanding, wide dissemination of knowledge, free and open discussion of available evidence, and dedication to expanded research.

In our recommendations in Volume I we argue for action to limit population growth now, based on the available evidence and the need to do something with the tools at our disposal to improve the conditions of life for families, by giving parents the means and the incentives to limit their fertility, and to help societies balance their numbers with available food, jobs, education, health services, or resources.

Rapid Population Growth follows two earlier Academy publications, *The Growth of World Population* (1963) and *The Growth of U.S. Population* (1965). It is an extension of our understanding and an expression of the

Academy's continuing sense of obligation to speak forthrightly on this most fundamental problem.

Our work contains statements of opinion as well as fact. We have drawn freely from our contributing authors and from the literature. We recognize that we have a certain bias stemming from our Judeo-Christian tradition and that controversy can surround many aspects of population questions, but our goal has been to approach our subject in a spirit of detachment and humane understanding of the wide range of values with which different societies approach these great issues.

We have attempted to offer policymakers reasoned options and to demonstrate the qualitative as well as the quantitative dimensions of human population change. Current research is accumulating evidence that considerations of individual and family welfare have a direct and immediate impact on the fertility behavior of parents. Equally critical are the long-term considerations of the total number of people in relation to total food supply, resources, land, and the environment that transcend several generations, because they too must be the concern of the planner and policymaker today.

We believe governments need to understand that quantitative and qualitative population questions are bound to force a series of increasingly far-reaching governmental policy decisions and that the longer these decisions are avoided, the more difficult they will become. Our goal is to contribute to the scientific analysis and informed opinion that can lead to intelligent policy formulation and execution in both the public and private sectors.

The Committee

Roger Revelle, Chairman
Ansley J. Coale
Moye Freymann
Oscar Harkavy
Hans Landsberg
Walsh McDermott

Norman Ryder
T. W. Schultz
George Stolnitz
Harold A. Thomas
Samuel Wishik
W. Murray Todd, Staff

Acknowledgments

Among the many people who have contributed to this study we wish to express our gratitude to the following: James W. Brackett, Philander Claxton, Arthur Devany, John Durand, Jason Finkle, Harald Frederiksen, Amos Hawley, Bert F. Hoselitz, Robert Hume, John Keppel, Howard J. Lewis, Juanita Mogardo, R. T. Ravenholt, Richard Reed, James Shannon, Alan Sweezy, Pauline Wyckoff, and George Zaidan.

A special note of thanks must go to Mrs. Carol Picard and Mrs. Sharon Bauer, who ably helped with the organization and production of the study, and Mrs. Jane Lecht, who edited our manuscripts.

Contents

VOLUME I
SUMMARY AND RECOMMENDATIONS

I

An Overview of the Problem

In this book we are concerned with the most fundamental event of our times—the enormous growth of the world's population during the last 3 decades, and the prospects for continued growth in the future. Many people believe, as Malthus did at first, though he later changed his mind, that the numbers of human beings will always increase up to a level set by the available food supply, or by enemies and disease. "Gigantic, inevitable famine stalks in the rear of misery and vice to limit the numbers of mankind." Even though death rates today are lower than they have ever been, and the proportion of the world's human population that is seriously malnourished is probably less than at any time since the Old Stone Age, the belief is widespread that uncontrolled population growth in the earth's poor countries is leading to catastrophe. It is possible, however, to take a different view, based on what we know about the history of human populations and on the behavior of many people at the present time—a view that social inventions will lead to a deliberate limitation of fertility by individual couples.

At the same time the technical potentialities exist, not only to feed all human beings, but greatly to improve the quality of human diets, at least until the end of this century. During the next 20 years no change in human fertility patterns can have much effect on the dimensions of the world food problem. And the natural resources available to present technology are sufficient to allow a vast improvement in the standard of living of all the people who will inhabit the earth 20 to 30 years from now. This is not to say that such an improvement in diets or standard of living will inevitably occur. It will depend on the improvement of social and economic institutions, and on the growth of cooperation and interdependence among the peoples of the world.

Nevertheless, a reduction in present rates of population growth is highly desirable from many points of view, because high fertility and rapid population growth have seriously adverse social and economic effects. A reduction in human fertility is an important component of social and economic development, although such a reduction cannot be a substitute for large capital investments and massive transfers of technology.

1

Rapid population growth has economic, social, and political effects. It also interacts with public education, health and welfare, and the quality of the environment in which people live. As we shall show, many of these consequences are not well understood, and their magnitude is uncertain. The significance of others is less than is generally believed. Without at this time assigning quantitative values, we may very briefly list the categories of consequences that are usually recognized. In later sections, these consequences are discussed more fully.

CATEGORIES OF CONSEQUENCES

Economic Consequences

Rates of population growth in many less developed countries are at least half the rates of economic growth and in some cases almost equal the latter. Chiefly because of the high fertility of these countries, the ratios of children to adults are very high when compared with these ratios in developed countries, and the numbers of young people reaching the age of labor force participation are rapidly increasing. Both of these factors produce serious economic consequences.

Rapid population growth slows down the growth of per capita incomes in less developed countries and tends to perpetuate inequalities of income distribution. It holds down the level of savings and capital investment in the means of production and thereby limits the rate of growth of gross national product. Food supplies and agricultural production must be greatly increased to meet the needs of rapidly growing populations, and this constrains the allocation of resources to other economic and social sectors. The number of persons entering the labor force grows very rapidly. Because the number of people seeking employment is larger than the number of available jobs, unemployment and underemployment are increasingly serious problems. An ever larger number of workers cannot be absorbed in the modern (industrialized) sector. They are forced into unproductive service occupations or back into the traditional (agricultural) sector with its low productivity and bare subsistence wage levels. Large supplies of cheap labor tend to hold back technological change, and industrialization is slowed by mass poverty, which reduces the demand for manufactured goods. Low savings rates and low labor skill inhibit the full development and utilization of natural resources in some countries, while in others the growing populations outrun the levels at which renewable resources can be sustained, and the resource base deteriorates. Widespread poverty, the low productivity of labor, the growing demands for food, and slow industrialization distort and degrade the international trade of the less developed countries.

Social Effects

Large-scale internal migration and rapid urbanization are among the most important social effects of rapid population growth. The growing numbers of children who survive their parents place new strains on intergenerational relationships. Social mobility is impeded by continuing widespread poverty. Because only a fraction of the growing population can be absorbed into the modern sector, the numbers of people in the traditional sector rapidly increase and the gap between the two continually widens. Thus two "nations," one relatively well off and the other backward and poor, exist side by side in the same country.

Political Effects

Political and social conflicts among different ethnic, religious, linguistic, and social groups are greatly worsened by rapid population growth. Political and administrative stresses are increased by the rural-urban migration which is partly caused by this growth, and by increasing demands for government services in health, education, welfare, and other functions. The large proportions of young people, particularly those who are unemployed or have little hope for a satisfactory future, form a disruptive and potentially explosive political force, although there is no evidence that rapid population growth is by itself the cause or even the major contributing factor in violence and aggression.

Consequences for Education

Because the numbers of children grow even more rapidly than the total population, the need for educating ever larger numbers inhibits the raising of enrollment ratios and improvement in the quality of education. High proportions of children reduce the amount out of any given educational budget that can be spent for the education of each child. Because each cohort, or age group, of the population is larger than its predecessor, it is difficult to recruit sufficient numbers of teachers from among the adult population.

Health, Welfare, and Child Development

The cost, adequacy, and nature of health and welfare services are affected by rapid population growth in much the same way as are those of educational services. In the individual family, maternal death and illness are increased by high fertility, early and frequent pregnancies, and the necessity of caring for excessive numbers of children. The physical and mental development of children is often retarded in large families because of inadequate nutrition and the diseases associated with poverty, and because the children are deprived of sufficient adult contact. Poor and crowded housing in the urban slums of rapidly growing cities produces further illness and retardation.

Environmental Deterioration

Necessarily rapid increases in agricultural production, both of crops and livestock, in many areas increase erosion, soil and water deterioration, and destruction of wildlife and natural areas. Pollution, caused by the indiscriminate use of pesticides, poisons people and domestic and wild animals.

EFFORTS TO SOLVE THE PROBLEM

Over a billion births will have to be prevented during the next 30 years to bring down the world's population growth rate from the present 2 percent per year to an annual rate of 1 percent by the year 2000. The task may well be the most difficult mankind has ever faced, for it involves the most fundamental characteristic of all life—the need to reproduce itself. An unprecedented effort is demanded, yet success will depend on the private actions of hundreds of millions of individual couples.

Until very recently, few nations had explicit population-influencing policies. Like the movement of a glacier, population changes were barely perceptible from year to year and yet were inexorable in character, seemingly beyond the range of government policy. Only within the last few years, when the vastly accelerated rates of population growth have become apparent to all, have governments recognized the needs and the possibility of actions to protect their people from the consequences of their own fertility and to effect reductions in fertility. Population policies are thus a new and untested area for politicians and administrators, who have neither tradition nor public consensus to guide them.

Nevertheless, many governments of developing countries are now adopting policies aimed at reducing birth rates and high rates of population growth. During the 1960's fifteen governments in Asia, nine in Africa, and fifteen in Latin America and the Caribbean area began to undertake fertility control programs, or to give support to unofficial programs in the absence of explicit formulation of government policy. The total population of the countries which have or support family planning programs is nearly 1,900 million, 80 percent of the population of the less developed world. Several of the rich countries, many intergovernmental agencies, and private foundations are providing financial help and expert advice for these fertility control programs.

This book is designed to stimulate planners and decision-makers of developed and developing nations to examine the consequences of rapid population growth for their own social and economic policies and patterns of action. That governments can and will take action we assume as the natural course of human affairs. Our goal is to encourage a thoughtful examination of the consequences of rapid population growth and their implications for public policy.

II

The Demographic Setting*

World population at the beginning of 1970 was over 3.5 billion. Less than two human generations ago, in 1930, it was 2 billion. About eleven generations ago, 1650—the onset of the modern era—it was only half a billion. In little more than one human generation hence, in the year 2000, world population could easily reach 7 billion and possibly greatly exceed this number. Growth rates have quickened: the world population increased from half a billion in 1650 to 1 billion in 1825, to 2 billion in 1930, and to 3 billion in 1960. If present rates continue, there will be 4 billion human beings by 1975. The acceleration is emphasized by calling attention to the ever shorter period required to double human numbers—175 years between 1650 and 1825, 105 years between 1825 and 1930, and 45 years between 1930 and 1975.

The public has become more and more aware of the dramatic rise in the rate of world population growth during the three centuries of the modern era. Rapid growth has been one of three related population phenomena generating acute public concern. The other two are the increasing concentration of the world's people on a relatively small proportion of the earth's surface—a phenomenon better known as urbanization and metropolitanization—and the growing diversity of the peoples who share the same geographic area and, increasingly, the same life space and the same economic, social, and political systems.

These three population developments are of relatively recent origin, spanning no more than about three of the perhaps forty thousand centuries that man or a close relative has resided on this planet. Only during the course of the present century have these three interrelated developments combined to generate world, national, and local crises, and to force intensified attention to population problems.

During the first three centuries of the modern era, from 1650 to 1950, world population multiplied about fivefold, from 0.5 to 2.5 billion, but over

---

*See the following chapters in Vol. II of this study: Philip M. Hauser, "World Population: Retrospect and Prospect"; Nathan Keyfitz, "Changes of Birth and Death Rates and their Demographic Effects"; and Dudley Kirk, "A New Demographic Transition?"

this time span the population of Europe (including the present Soviet Union) increased about sixfold, of Europe and European-occupied areas in the Western Hemisphere and Oceania combined, about eightfold. The population of northern America increased about 160-fold and that of Latin America about 14-fold.

During the same period the population of Asia increased by less than fourfold. (This contrasts with what must have been a much less rapid increase earlier. The *absolute* increases in Asia were very large.) In Africa, population merely doubled. It is clear that greatly accelerated growth occurred first among the nations that first experienced modernization–the combination of "revolutions," including the agricultural revolution, the commercial revolution, the industrial revolution, the science revolution, and the technological revolution. Explosive population growth, the "vital revolution"–a pace of growth without precedent in long-settled areas–did not approach present proportions among the two thirds of mankind in the developing nations in Asia, Latin America, and Africa until after World War I, and especially after World War II.

By the beginning of 1969 seven giant nations contained about three fifths of the world's peoples–some 2 billion. These nations are China with, perhaps, 730 million, India with 520 million, the Soviet Union with 240 million, the United States with 200 million, Pakistan with 130 million, Indonesia with 115 million, and Japan with 100 million.

Demographic Prospects

If present fertility rates persist and mortality trends continue, world population could reach 7.5 billion in the next 30 years. With reasonable allowance for reductions in fertility, world population could reach 7 billion by the century's end–perhaps the best estimate now possible on the assumption of no worldwide catastrophe such as a nuclear war. In the realm of the possible, also, is a world population considerably in excess of 7.5 billion if the growth rate continues to increase as it has done throughout this century.

In the shorter run, using the United Nations "high variant" population estimates giving a total of 7 billion by the turn of the century, world population will approximate 4 billion by 1975, 4.6 billion by 1980, 5 billion by 1985, and 5.7 billion by 1990. Almost certainly, the number will exceed 5.5 billion by 2000 because of the age composition of the present population. Potential parents are much more numerous than the present reproducing cohorts. These numbers underline the magnitudes of the problems that will face the world in the immediate future as population numbers continue to swell.

Between now and the century's end the developing nations are certain to experience higher growth rates than the economically advanced nations. By the year 2000, the now-developing areas may well number some 5.4 billion persons; the economically advanced nations, some 1.6 billion. Thus, while the modernized nations will increase by some 600 million during the next 30 years, the developing nations could increase by about 3 billion or five times as much.

The accelerating growth in human numbers is shown by comparing observed and projected annual increases. Between 1900 and 1950 the population of the world grew by some 20 million persons per year. On the basis of the projections we have cited, it could increase by an average of 90 million per year during the second half of this century, and by as much as 150 million per year during the first 20 years of the 21st century.

Birth Rates and Death Rates

World population growth is entirely the result of natural increase—the excess of births over deaths. For any subdivision of the world, net migration—the difference between out- and in-migration—is also a factor.

The population "explosion" is, in general, the result of great declines in death rates along with continuing high birth rates. When death rates began to fall, as they did in European populations in the 18th and 19th centuries, and in non-European populations in the 20th, more and more children survived to adulthood and were themselves able to produce children.

Among Europeans and populations of European stock, death rates declined rather slowly, requiring many decades to fall from 30-35 per 1,000 to the 15-20 per 1,000 typical of most less developed countries today.

Populations of European stock and, more recently, Japan have largely completed what demographers call the "demographic transition." Birth rates have declined from highs of 30 to 40 or more births per 1,000 population to below 20 per 1,000. Since death rates in these populations have now declined to the level of 10 per 1,000, annual growth rates are 1 percent or less, compared with 2 to 3.5 percent in less developed countries.

The great reductions in mortality did not reach the two thirds of mankind in the developing nations in Asia, Latin America, and Africa until after World War II. In general, birth rates have remained high, with the result that these areas are experiencing higher rates of natural increase than ever characterized the developed countries of today. Latin America, the most rapidly growing continental region, at 3 percent per year, will double its population in about 23 years.

The Recent Decline in Mortality in Less Developed Countries

The average expected lifetime at birth (life expectancy) for the population of India in 1910 was about 22 years, probably not much different from what it had been during the previous 2,000 years. For the less developed countries of Africa, Asia, and Latin America as a whole, life expectancy in the decade of the 1920's was probably less than 35 years, lower than it was in 1840 in western Europe, Canada, and the United States. An extremely rapid rise in life expectancy and a corresponding decline in death rates occurred during the first two decades after World War II, and is still continuing, though probably at a slower rate.

The reasons for this remarkable change are not entirely clear. One cause was certainly the widespread control and virtual elimination of malaria and some other insect-carried diseases. Others were the widespread use in rural areas of the less developed countries of vaccines and modern drugs, improved drinking water and sanitation, and better personal hygiene. All these public health measures, the products of modern technology, are relatively inexpensive and easy to use in the absence of much improvement in economic conditions. But improved nutrition resulting from greater abundance and better distribution of food supplies and some rise in per capita incomes have probably also been important factors in many regions. Famines on a widespread scale have been absent or infrequent owing to improved transportation and communications, and to greater concern for the welfare of the poor countries among food-surplus nations. There has been some speculation that human beings have developed more immunity to some microbial diseases or that the virulence of some microorganisms has declined. The period from the 14th to the 19th centuries has been called the "golden age of bacteria."

Recent Changes in Fertility in Some Less Developed Countries

In a few less developed countries there has been a significant decline in birth rates during the last 10 to 15 years. On the other hand, in at least some countries where birth rates are still high, these rates have apparently risen somewhat during recent years, probably because of greater survival and better health of mothers during their later reproductive years.

From 1960 to 1967 seven poor countries achieved declines in their birth rates of 20 to 35 percent: Taiwan, Hong Kong, Singapore, Mauritius, Barbados, Trinidad and Tobago, and Albania. Seven others showed declines of 12 to 19 percent: West Malaysia, Ceylon, Reunion, Jamaica, Puerto Rico, Chile, and Costa Rica. These rates of decline are much higher than those in the present developed countries during their period of demographic transition. Several other countries in Latin America seem to be approaching a point of fertility decline: Guyana, Venezuela, Panama, and Mexico.

In most of these countries there has been a substantial measure of economic development and, particularly, social change, including notable improvements in education, communication, social infrastructure, and life expectancy. Several of them have experienced a high per capita input of capital and technology from the rich countries. The evidence of these countries suggests that a certain "threshold" level of socioeconomic development may be a precondition for a sustained drop in birth rates. This threshold level differs rather substantially from region to region and from culture to culture, being lowest in the countries of Chinese culture on the eastern rim of Asia and much higher in Moslem cultures and the countries of Latin America.

Age Structure Patterns

Before the decline of mortality in western Europe the combination of high fertility and high mortality produced populations that tended to be relatively young, with an average age of about 25. Five or six children were born during the reproductive period of women, but of these only two or three survived to become adults. During the first stages of the demographic transition, as mortality—especially infant mortality—declined while fertility remained high, the average age of the population became lower and family size increased because larger proportions of children survived. Among the economically advanced nations, the presence of increased numbers of children probably contributed eventually to declines in the birth rate, especially in urban settings in which children tended increasingly to become an economic burden. Larger numbers of surviving children called for much more parental care, attention, and support, and also increased the need for community and national provisions for the young, including schools, health services, and recreation facilities.

As birth rates declined in what are now called the developed countries, the populations grew older and family size again became smaller. The median age of western populations rose to about 30, and the number of children ever born declined to two or three per family. The developing nations today, in contrast, still have predominantly young populations with growing family size because of increased child survival. Therefore, the burden of dependency is relatively high in these countries and increases in per capita income are retarded because the number of nonproducing consumers (both children and adults) is about as large as the number of workers.

Fertility, Mortality, and Changes in Family Size

As life expectancy goes up and death rates decline, the proportion of children less than 15 years old in the population increases, provided that the fertility rates remain constant, because fewer children die. For example, with six live births per woman, the percentage of children goes from 39 percent when life expectancy is 30 years to 45 percent with a life expectancy of 60 years, an increase of about 28 percent in the child/adult ratio. The average number of children under 15 in each family increases in the same proportion. However, the effect of changes in death rates on the proportion of children and on family size is much smaller than the effect of an equal change in birth rates. The principal demographic effect of rapid population growth resulting from a high and nearly constant birth rate and a low death rate–as contrasted with a nearly stationary population having both a high birth rate and a high death rate–is that the number of families in each generation is very much larger than in the preceding generation. This situation has serious consequences for a rural society with a limited supply of arable land, because it means that the size of farms for each family greatly diminishes from one generation to the next.

THREE POPULATION TYPES IN LESS DEVELOPED COUNTRIES

We may divide the less developed countries at the present time into three groups on the basis of their population patterns: (1) countries with both high birth rates and high death rates; (2) countries with high birth rates and low death rates; and (3) countries with intermediate and declining birth rates and low death rates. The first group consists of those countries, most in Africa and some in Asia, in which per capita incomes are extremely low and the process of modernization has barely begun. Probably only a few hundred million people are in this group. Most of the less developed countries in Asia and Latin America, and some in Africa–in all containing nearly 2 billion people–are in the second group. The third consists of a few countries on the fringe of Asia and in Latin America, in several of which there has been a marked improvement in economic and social conditions during the last 2 decades.

In the high-birth-rate, high-death-rate countries the life expectancy is about equal to that of Sweden in 1800, but birth rates are about 50 percent higher and the rate of population growth several times as great as in Sweden 170 years ago. (See Table 1.) In Honduras and Taiwan, which are, respectively, examples of the second and third groups of countries, the death rates are lower than in Sweden in 1966, because of their very young population, even though their life expectancies are less than the Swedish. Birth rates are 2 to 3 times as high, and rates of population growth 4.5 to 6 times greater in Taiwan and Honduras than in Sweden today. There is about one adult for every child under 15 in all three groups of less developed countries, in contrast to nearly four adults per child in Sweden in 1966.

Possible Future Increase in Rates of Population Growth

In the coming years it is possible that population growth rates in developing areas will continue to increase, even after declines in fertility rates begin, for continued declines in mortality may more than offset declines in fertility for some time. World population growth rates will continue to increase if decreases in growth rates in economically advanced areas are more than offset

TABLE 1

Three Population Patterns in Less Developed Countries
Compared with Sweden in 1800 and 1966

	High Birth Rates High Death Rates Average, 22 African Countries	High Birth Rates Low Death Rates, Honduras, 1966	Intermediate Birth Rates Low Death Rates, Taiwan, 1966	Sweden 1800	Sweden 1966
Average population, millions	4.5	2.36	12.79	2.35	7.81
Birth rate/1,000	47.8	44.2	32.5	31	15.8
Death rate/1,000	26.1	8.7	5.5	26	10
Rate of increase/1,000	21.7	35.5	27	5	5.8
Doubling time, years	32	20	26	140	120
Life expectancy, years	37.1	60	64	38	74
Percent less than 15 years old	42.9	51	43.5	33	21
Density, persons per hectare	0.13	0.12	3.56	0.05	0.17

Sources: *United Nations Demographic Yearbook, 1966.* New York, 1969; Nathan Keyfitz, "Changes in Birth and Death Rates and Their Demographic Effects," Annex in Vol. 2 of this study.

by acceleration in the less developed areas. Furthermore, the advanced countries that experienced a postwar baby boom are likely to undergo a rise in birth rate during the coming years as an echo-effect of the first boom, and their population growth rates may, therefore, also increase.

DENSITY AND DEVELOPING NATIONS

Density as such is not an indicator of overpopulation. The density of population per unit of total land area in most less developed countries of Asia is less than the density in western Europe and Japan, whereas the density in the large countries of Africa and Latin America is about the same as that in such "empty" countries as the United States and the Soviet Union. Except for Taiwan and Egypt, which are exceptionally crowded, the density on cultivated land in all less developed countries is about the same as in western Europe. Most of the countries of Africa and Latin America contain large areas of arable but uncultivated land, but in Asia most land that could be cultivated has already been put under the plow. Modern high-yielding agricultural technology and fertility limitation must be introduced and expanded in these Asian countries if diets are to be improved or even if all people are to be fed in the future. (See Table 2.)

URBANIZATION

From 45 percent to 90 percent of the populations of the poor countries live in rural areas, but the rate of growth of cities in these countries exceeds their overall rate of population growth. For example, between 1950 and 1960, in twenty-four countries with per capita incomes of less than $250 per year, cities of more than 100,000 inhabitants grew 60 percent more rapidly than the total population. The average rate of growth of these large cities was over 4 percent per year; they were doubling in population every 17 years. The excess growth of cities was due to migration from the countryside, in part as a result of the diminishing size of farms and the increasing difficulties in making a living in rural areas. Although living conditions for many migrants in the cities are appallingly bad, they are probably better, from several points of view, than in the villages.

DESIRED AND ACTUAL NUMBERS OF CHILDREN

Sample surveys of both urban and rural people in less developed countries show that a high proportion of couples having four or more living children do not want any more. The best current data strongly suggest that, on the average, the number of live births exceeds by one or two children the number

TABLE 2

Population Densities in Certain Developed
and Less Developed Countries

	Population 1965	Total Area	Cultivated Area	Density on Total Area	Density on Cultivated Land
	Millions	Millions of Hectares		Persons/Hectare	
LESS DEVELOPED COUNTRIES					
People's Republic of China	730	956	145	0.7	5
India	483	304	162	1.6	3
Pakistan	115	95	29	1.2	4
Indonesia	105	149	18	0.7	5.8
Philippines	32	30	11	1.1	2.9
Thailand	31	51	10	0.6	3.1
Republic of China (Taiwan)	12	3.6	1	3.3	12
Ceylon	11	6.6	2	1.7	5.5
Ghana	8	24	5	0.3	1.6
Madagascar	6	59	3	0.1	2
Tanzania	11	94	9	0.1	1.2
United Arab Republic	30	100	3	0.3	10
Mexico	41	197	11	0.2	3.7
Brazil	81	851	19	0.1	4.3
Colombia	16	114	5	0.1	3.2
DEVELOPED COUNTRIES					
Soviet Union	234	2240	230	0.1	1
United States	195	936	185	0.2	1
Japan	98	37	6	2.7	16.3
France	49	55	21	0.9	2.2
West Germany	57	25	8	2.3	7.1
United Kingdom	54	24	7	2.2	7.7

Sources: (col. 1) *Population Reference Bureau Data Sheet*. Washington, D.C., December 1965; (col. 2) United Nations *Demographic Yearbook, 1965*. New York, 1966; (cols. 3, 5) United Nations Food and Agricultural Organization, *Production Yearbook*, Vol. 23, 1969. Rome, 1969. Col. 4 calculated from cols. 1 and 2.

desired. One reason is probably the high infant and child mortality in the less developed countries. Out of five or six live births, the probabilities are high that one or two children will die. For any individual family there is a large degree of uncertainty about the survival of their children. The excess children over the number desired can be thought of as a kind of insurance against this uncertainty. Moreover, though infant and child mortalities have been reduced in the last few years, people still remember the past high death rates for children. For example, in the Matlab region in East Pakistan, the average woman 45 years old has given birth to 7.6 children; 2.6, or 34 percent, of

these children have died. Today 21 percent die. Another important reason for
the excess of live births over the number of desired children is undoubtedly
the ineffectiveness, difficulty, and hardship of preventing births with the
methods now available to the people of the poor countries. This is a powerful
argument for family planning programs; but even if these programs were
completely successful in eliminating unwanted births, the desired number of
children in most less developed countries is so high that rapid population
growth would still occur.

WHAT GOVERNMENTS ARE DOING

The governments of developing countries are now adopting population
control policies at a rate and in a climate of world approval unimaginable
even a few years ago. Among the nations that have officially decided to foster
family planning are Ceylon, People's Republic of China, Republic of China
(Taiwan), India, Indonesia, Iran, South Korea, Malaysia, Nepal, Pakistan, the
Philippines, Singapore, Thailand, Turkey, Ghana, Kenya, Mauritius, Morocco,
Tunisia, Egypt, Puerto Rico, Jamaica, Trinidad and Tobago, and Fiji. In many
other countries at least the beginning of governmental interest and support is
visible: for example, Hong Kong, Dahomey, Gambia, Nigeria, Barbados,
Chile, Colombia, Costa Rica, Cuba, Dominican Republic, El Salvador, Ecua-
dor, Honduras, Nicaragua, Panama, and Venezuela.

The role of governments in reducing fertility is to exhort, inform, and
provide; decisions and actions must be taken by individual couples acting in
accordance with their perceived interests. Even so, the governmental task is
large and difficult, requiring a high degree of organization, adequate financial
and logistic support, great flexibility in meeting changing conditions, and
continuing objective evaluation of results.

Only a small proportion of people in the less developed countries have
even moderately good knowledge of modern methods of family planning; the
poor and the uneducated need to learn what the well-to-do and the educated
already know—that there are a number of safe, reliable, and simple ways of
limiting one's family. Knowledge of contraceptive methods is much rarer than
the desire not to have more children.

Another task of governments of developing countries is to find, to learn
how to bring about, and to help individual families to recognize the changes
in living conditions that lower the economic, social, and psychic benefits and
increase the costs of having more than two or three children. Research is also
needed to develop methods of fertility control that are easier to introduce

*Berelson, Bernard, "The Present State of Family Planning Programs," Paper pre-
sented at Conference on Technological Change and Population Growth at the California
Institute of Technology, May 1970.

than the present oral contraceptives and mechanical devices. Much of this research can be done by the developed nations.

One by one, explicitly or implicitly, governments are actively assisting or deliberately allowing the extension of means and information to facilitate planning of family size by individual couples. For example, India and Pakistan have now deployed about one family planning worker for every 1,000 families. The U.S. Government has budgeted first $3 million, then $35 million, and ultimately $100 million in the last few years to contribute to the extension of family planning to those who need and want it in the less developed countries. Similarly, the U.S. Government budgeted $24.4 million, $55 million, and $80.6 million from 1967 to 1969 for family planning, research, and training in the United States.

Foundations and international nongovernmental organizations (including the Ford and Rockefeller Foundations, the Population Council, and the International Planned Parenthood Federation) have been particularly instrumental in catalyzing the development of national policies and programs. In many countries in which no explicit national population policies and no overt national population programs exist, there are nongovernmental associations demonstrating, in both the utilization and extension of family planning services, that family planning is respectable, beneficial, and desirable.

III

The Consequences of
Rapid Population Growth

In thinking about the consequences of rapid population growth, it is useful to consider both the kinds of effects and the nature of the causes, whether these be the speed of growth itself, the underlying high birth rates, or population size and density. We are also concerned with the time spans over which the effects occur, and the scale; that is, whether we are dealing with a country or a region as a whole, or with the level of the family, village, community, or other small social unit.

In the discussion that follows we begin with the concern about adequacy of resources.

RESOURCES*

Public concern over the adequacy of resources to meet the demands of a rapidly growing population advances and recedes; it never ceases, and for good reason. The arithmetical exercise that pits rising demand against a stock of resources that, in some ultimate sense, is physically finite though inadequately known, is both easy to perform and, for many, hard to resist. The dismal outcome is a foregone conclusion, provided the time horizon is sufficiently extended. Demand projections have an apparent persuasiveness, even when carried into the distant future, that is not matched by projections of supply which must be based on conservative assumptions if they are not to appear highly speculative. Projections of demand thus "swamp" projections of supply, and a crisis is predicted within easily specified time ranges.

The missing ingredient in this type of prognostication is the ability to measure man's capacity to manipulate the kind and volume of the resources he uses (including his ability to meet specific shortages of materials, the way in which he manages resource exploitation, and his control over his own numbers).

Providing for the required resources seems overwhelmingly difficult when we look into the future, and yet, looking backward, we learn that man seems

*See Joseph L. Fisher and Neal Potter, "The Effects of Population Growth on Resource Adequacy and Quality," in Vol. II of this study.

not to have failed, certainly not as disastrously as the forward look often presages. Specifically, mankind has not "run out" of any critical resources. Working through the market and the play of prices that operate on both demand and supply, costs of primary resources have not risen relative to other goods and services. In many instances they have fallen, and yet larger numbers of people now not only live longer but also enjoy higher standards of living, however measured, than were open to their forebears.

Management and Resources

Not surprisingly, the complexity of the resources issue has given rise to two basic schools of thought: One is inclined to take a very long view and doubts that technology can be relied upon to help extend resources at a pace to stay abreast of population growth; the other infers from the history of the past hundred years or so that science and technology can provide the basis for new discoveries (e.g., ore bodies, fuel deposits) and substitutes (e.g., petrochemicals, nuclear energy) to keep a step ahead of the "Malthusian trap." But not even the most ardent adherents of the second school argue that, without reduction and ultimate leveling off of the rate of population growth, the Malthusian proposition can be dismissed (short, that is, of a total recycling of all depletable materials).

Neither of the two approaches is as clear-cut as here stated. For example, leaving aside discoveries and substitution, much can be gained from more rational management of supplies of resources. The same piece of soil, managed differently, can be the basis for vastly differing rates of agricultural output. Identical deposits can be made to yield greatly varying supplies of fuel. Rational management is a prime variable in the sustainable yield of a given stand of timber. And so on.

Though less obvious, management is just as important in affecting the demand for resources. "Wastefulness" is usually identified with specific techniques or conditions associated with production or output, but its implications on the demand side, though less noted, are no less notable. Production subsidies that stimulate consumption beyond the point to which it would be carried if prices reflected true costs are a common example.

More recently, a subtle but specific case of subsidization has come to plague the high income countries particularly. "Environmental pollution" results, in one of its major manifestations, from the failure of prices to reflect the social costs that producers (and thus also consumers) are able to impose on society as a whole. Typically this pollution is in the form of liquid or gaseous effluents, but it can also take other forms with adverse impacts on the landscape, living things, or other facets of the environment. These social costs are paid in a context removed from their origins. When prices do not reflect them, partially or fully, certain products are in a very real sense priced below their true costs, and demand for them is greater than it would be under conditions of full cost allocation.

Finally, people are neither mechanical robots nor fruit flies in their reproductive behavior. Parents the world over tend to behave over their lifetimes as if they were rational economic persons. Children entail costs and they provide satisfactions and returns. Parents tend to try to have an economically optimal number of children. In poor countries one reason for present high birth rates is that, in a very real sense, children are the poor man's capital.

The Role of Population and Income Growth in Resource Demand

Aggregate demand for resources is the product of per capita income and numbers of people. The relative roles of these two factors differ over time, between regions and countries, and in their impact on quantity and quality aspects of demands for different resources. In countries characterized by high income and low or moderate population growth, the effect of rising income in most situations outweighs that of rising numbers, often substantially, and the impact of high income is greater on quality than on quantity. That is to say, despite rising population, these nations have had only relatively transitory problems in procuring their material resources, by and large at constant cost and in some instances even at declining cost.

Rising incomes have triggered a vast expansion of durable goods mainly powered by mechanical energy, and nondurables designed to ease the burden of daily routines. Their joint effect has been not to create material scarcities, as was feared by some economists at the turn of the century and quite generally in the decade following World War II, but, as the ecologists had warned, to strain the capacity of the environment to absorb both the products that have served their purpose and the unintended by-products or residuals resulting from production, distribution, and consumption.

Income, rather than *number*, of consumers has been the more important factor in producing pollution. Analysis of historical data reveals that increases in aggregate energy consumption are caused to the extent of about two thirds by rising per capita consumption, i.e. income, and one third by rising population; and this appears to be as true in high income countries like the United States or the United Kingdom as in India or other low income countries. Especially striking is electricity generation, which is an important source of air pollution. In the past 30 years or so, 10 percent, at most, of the growth of electricity consumption can be attributed to population increase.

Human numbers as such have been a potent factor in aggravating the problem of maintaining privacy, or simply elbow room, which for a growing share of the population is harder to find. But even here, income is a factor. Rising per capita income, compounded by increased leisure time and more rapid transportation facilities, has spread congestion from the city—where it is always present but where larger and larger parts of the population elect to live—to the nonurban landscape and most notably to recreation areas such as parks and beaches.

The situation so far has been quite different in less developed countries, where food claims half and more of a family's expenditure (surveys in India put it at 60 to 70 percent) and the elasticity of the demand for food is high. Because of the low levels of income in developing countries, even relatively rapid increases in per capita income have not in the aggregate put much pressure on nonfood resources. Food is a nonpostponable necessity of life for which there is no substitute, and because it absorbs such a large share of family income, it has always been the most critical resource problem.

At the same time, the rising demand for more and better food, which comes from both increased numbers and rising income, has pressed hard against land and water resources. To the extent that food becomes more widely available, expenditure patterns will change. Rising income will have increasing impact, and attention will shift from adequacy of food, land, and water to other resources, and unless the developing nations take extraordinary care, pollution will accompany these changes.

The Resource Future

From a worldwide view, divergent resource utilization and population trends suggest that, to the end of the century and probably beyond, there is sufficient promise in technology to assure the availability of resources, especially when technology is assisted by management to minimize wastefulness and maximize efficiency. Even for the short run, however, the confidence about resource adequacy in high income countries cannot hold for the poorer ones. Given the grossly unequal geographic distribution of many resources, optimism would be justified only if each country were endowed with enough nonresource-based earning capacity to obtain by trade what it cannot obtain by production. Adequate data on which to make such assessments are not available, and it is impossible to judge whether the resource position of each country will be analogous to that of the world as a whole. The fragmentary or episodic evidence that exists leads one to believe that the answer is negative. After all, although trade fills the gap in resource endowment, each country needs something to trade. That "something" is in many instances not readily apparent.

To illustrate, Fisher and Potter (see Volume II of this report) speculate on the magnitude of energy consumption by the end of the century. By assuming a continuing rising 10-year trend (1955-65), noncommunist Asia's energy consumption could reach 10 billion tons of coal-equivalent by the year 2000. At that level the area would enjoy a per capita consumption about 10 percent above the level prevailing in western Europe in 1965. But this coal-equivalent of energy is about five times the aggregate consumption of North America in 1965, which was associated with a GNP of almost $750 billion. Assuming a pretty close correlation between GNP and energy consumption, the 10 billion tons of coal would be indicative of a GNP ranging between $3,500 and $4,000 billion. In 1965, the GNP of noncommunist Asia was $230 billion; thus the annual growth rate between 1965 and 2000 would have to be between 8 and 9 percent to make such a projection of energy consumption believable—a wholly unlikely event.

World energy resources could, in all likelihood, meet even this doubtful level of demand, but the prospective costs stagger the imagination. In financial terms, 1965 energy consumption was equivalent to almost $4 billion for the Asian area. For the hypothetical projection in 2000, the bill would be more nearly $100 billion—implying a demand for foreign exchange that can be produced only by exports and tourism. Thus, a reassuring global, physical outlook about resources (as Fisher and Potter caution) requires one to pay scant attention to geographic differences and the ability to pay.

In speculating about resource adequacy one can, on the other hand, easily be led to a much more pessimistic view than circumstances suggest. Exceedingly pessimistic projections can be, and have been, made by compounding projected world population with current per capita resource use in developed countries. Whereas this may serve to highlight the outer limits of conditions that could some day prevail, it is well to keep in mind that (a) such a development would occur only in association with levels of per capita income now prevailing in high income countries but which, as indicated above, are unlikely to be reached for a great many decades; and (b) there is little reason to believe that the mix of materials in these countries will in any way parallel that prevailing in the developed countries. On the contrary, it is quite likely, for example, that developing countries will skip the "coal and steel age" and take off into the chemical, and later into the nuclear, age at much earlier stages of their development than they would if they approximated the historical sequences of the developed countries.

The probability is small that the less developed countries will be in any way carbon copies, in their materials usage, of western Europe or North America. From this view, assessing the capacity of any specific country or area to obtain needed resources may yield in time quite different and perhaps more encouraging results. By implication, such considerations also put in a different light the often-voiced complaint that the high income countries, most prominently the United States, account for only a small share of the world's population but consume a major share of annual raw materials production. Apart from the fact that such consumption represents, in foreign trade, a major source of income for the exporting countries, it is quite possible that many resources will lose significance in the future, particularly as changes in relative prices influence the impetus toward substitution. Finally, there is every reason to believe that the final third of the 20th century will witness a great improvement in recycling of waste and thus depress the demand for new material, as well as open to question the conventional supply-demand resource balances.

Resources and Trade

The effects of rapid population growth on postwar world trade have been substantial and, on the whole, adverse to the developing countries. Among these effects have been steady erosion of exportable surpluses (i.e., surpluses in a market sense, not surpluses over amounts that would be required to provide satisfactory levels of living for everybody regardless of ability to pay) and the transformation of many less developed countries from large net exporters to large net importers, especially of food.

This transformation was due primarily to the fact that rising demands for food were not matched by proportionate increases in production. It took place not because larger portions of domestic production went into improved consumption levels, but because rapidly rising numbers of people had to be supplied with basic requirements, with little improvement in per capita quantity or quality of production. Unhappily it also coincided with the emergence of competing—generally man-made—materials developed in the industrialized countries. There was a reduction in the size of export markets for such commodities as rubber, fats and oil, fibers, leather, etc.; and the potential for substitution has by no means been exhausted.

The last few years, however, have opened up a different prospect. Recent advances in the agricultural performance of several less developed countries, briefly mentioned earlier, are altogether likely—perhaps by the mid-1970's—to produce commercial surpluses of food, especially grains. The Philippines is the first country to move into this situation. Pakistan hopes to join soon, as do others. To the extent that they do, the immediate effect—though dampened by the outlays for fertilizer, other chemicals, machinery, etc. required to achieve the new levels of output—can relieve the hitherto adverse trade and foreign exchange situations of those countries if donor-nation aid policies and competition are favorable.

The volume of future grain exports will depend upon the extent to which governments will want, or be able, to favor exports over domestic consumption of either grain or animal products. This policy involves not only efforts to supplement the purchasing power of the poor but also an account of the effect of increasing urbanization on food demand. The expected effect of urbanization is increased demand on the organized food market, and eventually on the whole economy, through rising incomes. None of these contingencies, however, can obscure the principal new fact that additional food supplies are increasing the options.

Whether the aspirations of the newly emerging exporters will run into heavy competition in world markets, given the large unexploited production potential of traditional exporters from developed countries, is another unanswerable question.

ECONOMIC CONSEQUENCES*

Public and professional attention to the economic consequences of population change tends to cluster about two poles of emphasis. One, crisis oriented, focuses on the possibility of systemwide disaster; famine, depletion of natural resources, and other ecological threats have been linked to population growth at least since the time of Malthus. The second pole of attention concentrates on the interrelationships between demographic and economic trends.

The word "crisis" is often attached to developments that are suddenly perceived but have long been in existence. Conversely, some economic-demographic trends are not called crises because they are unobtrusive or continuous; yet they may involve greater social burdens—or at least are more directly related to population—than do threats of "breakdown." For example, the social and economic costs from impaired maternal and child health resulting from high fertility may outweigh in welfare terms any probable threat of starvation or ecological collapse.

In analyzing the economic effects of population growth, it is important to distinguish between developed countries and much less developed countries. A minimum distinction in economic-geographic terms would separate most of Europe, the United States, Canada, Oceania, Japan, and a very few other countries from most of Latin America, Asia, and Africa, although a number of European-settled economies and subeconomies in these latter three regions may be classed as developed. With few exceptions, the developed nations are characterized by relatively long (50 years or more) histories of development, high incomes (with recent per capita gross national products, or GNP's, of about $1,000 as a crude but helpful dividing mark), and low fertility (birth rates of below 20 to 25 per 1,000 as an upper boundary).

The less developed regions, by contrast, have with few exceptions brief histories of development; current per capita incomes in the $100-$600 range (most being under $400 and those between $600 and $1,000 being more akin to newly developing areas than to developed areas in terms of basic economic structure and other indicators of modernization); and birth rates well above

*See the chapters in Vol. II of this study by Paul Demeny, Dudley Kirk, Harvey Leibenstein, T. Paul Schultz, and Theodore W. Schultz.

30 per 1,000 and commonly more than 40 per 1,000, which are more than double that of the developed regions.

In the less developed countries, and particularly in their predominant agrarian sectors, the main economic effects of rapid population growth are on supply; productive capabilities and capacities are more limited and population growth rates are very high. In the developed countries, with their moderately fluctuating demographic factors and high productive potential, the main effects of demographic changes are on demand; the main question usually is whether productive capacity will be utilized rather than whether it is large enough.

Food—the Crisis That Has Not Materialized

In the developed regions, the impact of population growth on food supply needs has been limited for many decades and promises to continue on a "non-crisis" path indefinitely into the future. In contrast to the developing regions, the main elements are moderate to low rates of population growth, high and rising domestic food production capacities, adequate and expanding capabilities for obtaining food imports as needed, and the fact that food consumption varies much less than proportionately with per capita income. Furthermore, rates of population change in developed countries have generally been declining for over a decade and long-term declines in the future seem more likely than increases.

In the less developed regions, on the other hand, the need for cautious or even ambiguous forecasts has been demonstrated vividly in recent years. Fears of massive famine or at least growing threats of spreading starvation, expressed by numerous competent observers until very recently, have been abruptly succeeded by a largely contrary, equally substantial, and informed consensus.

Given all due precautions, the record and the main overall prospects are noteworthy, even startling. Widespread famine that could reasonably be attributed to economic incapability has not been observed in any of the less developed regions for decades. Fear of famine reached a peak in the mid-1960's, largely as a result of crop failure in parts of Asia coupled with dwindling international food reserves. These fears have been allayed by the elimination of recent shortages and the prospects for a long-run sharp upward trend in output of food grains.

The change in expert opinion seems to have stemmed from the agricultural turnabout in India, where 2 years of severe droughts have been suddenly followed by what many informed observers regard as a confirmed "Green Revolution."

Previous declines in international food reserves have been superseded by very large and rapid build-up of surpluses, which in any event have always been mainly a matter of policy in the high income areas and not of resource limitations as such. In the less developed countries, despite their very different basic resource position, agricultural policy has been reassessed as a prime mover of modernization and expanding output, which governments can manipulate at their option. Agricultural research and development have been encouraged and subsidized. Price incentives have helped to accelerate technical innovation and increased production by cultivators. Public policy has assigned higher priorities to providing irrigation water, new varieties of seed, and fertilizer. As a result, a trend toward food self-sufficiency is observed in a growing number of low income countries that previously were dependent on imports. In the opinion of many today, the world's food supply prospects have taken a radical turn for the better, at least for the next decade or two. Indeed, attention is now directed at problems of agricultural surplus. There are fears that export earnings will decrease as previously importing areas become more, or entirely, self-sufficient; that increased output in modern agrarian sectors will further depress the subsistence sectors by forcing down prices; and that increased landlessness and other "push" forces operating in the countryside will add to the already enormous social and economic costs of accommodating the flow of people to urban areas.

In short, fears of food supply disasters in the less developed countries seem less sustainable today than at perhaps any time in the last 25 years. Quite apart from the dramatic nature of the recent turnabout in the world food-population picture, the avoidance of any major disaster from economic causes would be noteworthy on other grounds. For one, it has been achieved in the face of unprecedentedly steep, and still rising, rates of population growth, involving rates and numbers today which are something like double or more those encountered in the less developed countries only 30 to 40 years ago. Although trends in food consumption per capita are too poorly documented to permit generalization for any substantial part of the less developed countries, such data as there are on calorie and protein intake suggest that increases since the 1930's have not been uncommon, though with a number of important exceptions and with many more instances of shorter-run fluctuations or declines since the 1950's.

Whatever the actual facts in the documented cases and the many more undocumented ones, the trends in food consumption have clearly not impeded remarkable gains in longevity and disease control. (That they have been causes of such gains in any significant degree seems doubtful in most instances.) Death rates have fallen and life expectancy has risen spectacularly throughout nearly all Latin America and Asia and many parts of Africa—often at rates of change with no precedent in the recorded annals of the developed regions.

Despite the prevalence of high rural population density in many less developed countries, their trends in agricultural output have been remarkably resistant to the adverse impacts of added numbers. For the less developed regions as a whole, growth rates of output between the mid-1950's and mid-1960's (i.e., before the Green Revolution) averaged between 2.5 and 3 percent per annum, a respectable level both by historical standards and the contemporary performance in developed regions. Nor has this been a recent or anomalous occurrence. Between the 1930's and 1950's, growth in food output within the less developed regions was again impressive by both historical and comparative guidelines, though, of course, it was accompanied by slower rates of population growth and less pressure on the agrarian sector.

Negative Effects of Rapid Population Growth. However, if we view the world food picture in terms of reciprocal effects of economic and demographic trends—granted that neither crisis nor disaster seems likely—a very different outlook emerges. Per capita food production in the less developed countries remained practically unchanged between the mid-1950's and mid-1960's in spite of substantial increases in total output. In the developed regions, on the other hand, per capita output increased significantly. Analysis of the actual output trends in the less developed countries shows that per capita production could have been approximately one sixth higher than was actually the case for 1965, had their population growth rates been those of the developed regions.

The less developed countries' output growth rates, despite their impressive level, came to only about two thirds or three fourths of the United Nations Food and Agricultural Organization Indicative World Plan objectives, and the entire amount of the shortfall could have been overcome by no more than a limited downtrend in fertility from traditional toward more modern levels—for example, from the present average of some 40 per 1,000 to 25 or 30 per 1,000.

Agricultural performance in the less developed countries continues to be highly subject to the vagaries of climate and weather. Sudden drops in food supply, which are usually accompanied by falling effective demand in the farm sector, reduced domestic saving, and worsened balance of payments, can spell the difference between substantial growth and stagnation in whole economies. New technology has partly countervailed the wind and weather, but the vulnerability of most less developed countries to such "exogenous" factors has not yet been significantly reduced, even where, as in India, the probability of longer-run agricultural progress seems substantial.

The main effects of agricultural transformation in the less developed countries could be relatively sudden spurts in output rather than a permanent upkink in trend from, for example, the recent 2 to 3 percent increase per year to a 4 to 5 percent annual increase persisting indefinitely into the future. Should this happen, continued population growth at current rates could, even if temporarily exceeded by output advances, again begin to dominate the food-population balance—and negatively—in the longer run. Rapid population growth could threaten the adequacy of the food supply after a period, say, by 1980 or 1990.

At the least, there has now begun a period of perhaps 2 decades during which providing a country's minimum food requirements will not necessarily have the attributes of a daily crisis. But what is *possible* is by no means *assured*. Success with the new varieties depends on the ability of farmers to obtain irrigation water, fertilizers, pesticides, seeds, farm tools, and eventually machinery, transportation, storage, and new knowledge. To be able to make the necessary purchases, farmers will have to sell a fraction of their crops. This presupposes either considerable growth in domestic incomes, especially outside the agricultural sector—i.e., overall economic development—or the availability of export markets.

For food supplies in the long run, only the first alternative seems significant for the developing countries in general. A scramble among newly export-oriented producers to supply the needs of similarly situated and motivated countries is not likely to bring rewards to all. Nor, on the other hand, is encroachment upon the markets of the traditional grain exporters of the world, domestic or foreign, a likely prospect; and the markets for specialized agricultural exports—sugar, coffee, tea, rubber, bananas, cocoa, jute, and similar products—from the poor countries to the rich hold out few prospects of sufficient growth. Some may even decline, particularly when they are vulnerable to substitution. In summary, although the technology is at hand for a large increase in agricultural production and farmers have demonstrated their capacity for adopting it, there is a serious question whether the necessary economic conditions to sustain this trend may be attained or sustained, quite apart from troublesome social and political by-products the trend may create—in human resources, social stability, and effects on the environment.

Increased agricultural productivity eventually results in lower food prices, to the benefit of consumers. Over any decade, however, a *consumer surplus* necessarily becomes smaller per consumer when it is distributed among the rapidly increasing numbers of consumers produced by rapid population growth.

There are also questions concerning whether incomes will rise fast enough to absorb rapidly rising farm output, either directly or in the form of livestock products; whether the lower prices needed for market-clearing will tend to discourage the innovators; whether new government taxes on inputs or income will dampen enthusiasm; or whether sufficient funds will be available to continue the expansion of irrigated areas.

Some observers have conjectured that the capital investments for the economic development that must occur to sustain the agricultural transformation, both for needed inputs and markets, will require much larger capital inflows in the future. The Pearson Committee,* for example, advocates

*See *Partners in Development, Report of the Commission on International Development,* Chairman: Lester B. Pearson. New York: Praeger, 1969. pp. 143-148.

raising the rate of growth of economic development to 6 percent by 1975 and judges that this will require a flow of external resources equal to 1 percent of the GNP's of the rich countries—nearly a doubling of current aid. Although the 1 percent "target" may seem an arbitary notion chosen for its simplicity, the Pearson Committee reports that, according to studies now being conducted by a U.N. committee, the amounts thus transferred would not be inconsistent with what might be called "requirements" in the less developed countries. It is clear that continuation of recent rates of population growth is likely to shape internal needs in the poor countries in ways that will postpone desirable changes in trade, consumption, and investment patterns.

Agricultural transformations in the less developed countries not only affect food production and consumption but also will profoundly affect the distribution of overall income and assets. Land-tenure patterns, distributions of agrarian incomes and farm holdings by size, and rates of rural-urban migration are likely to be significantly modified. In all these respects, rapid population growth seems certain to increase the number of landless, subsistence, or disadvantaged peasantry and to raise the administrative burdens and social costs of absorbing urban arrivals. Conversely, a slower population growth could lessen the severity of these effects, once its cumulative influence on numbers began to take effect.

Economywide Effects of Rapid Population Growth

A macro view of demographic-economic interactions in the less developed countries, using overall income aggregates rather than food proper, leads to remarkably similar judgments. Unprecedented and still accelerating population growth has not prevented very rapid economic advance. Population growth, though not a negligible block to development and modernization, has also not been an overriding factor.

Increases in GNP during the 1950's and again in the 1960's were at rates which have just about matched the contemporary rates in the developed regions; they accelerated between the two decades, and they ranged well beyond the magnitudes recorded for the industrializing nations of the 19th century. Although much of the information about individual nations is subject to error, it would be surprising if the correct facts, were they known, would overturn the broad conclusions. By both comparative and historical standards, economic growth in less developed countries has been remarkably rapid, despite record population growth and its anticipated handicaps to development through reduced savings potentials, increased consumption needs, added imports and reduced supplies of foreign exchange, or lagging investment per unit of labor.

Among individual less developed countries, moreover, the relation between income (gross domestic product) and rates of population growth has been low during the 1950's and again in the 1960's. The statistical relations are, if anything, positive in each case.

Much the same patterns have held for the developed economies during the postwar decades. Here, however, one would expect population growth to have a positive impact on economic growth, since growth in the developed countries increases demand under conditions of high productive capacity.

To summarize, recent differential rates of change in productive performance have not been obviously related empirically to rates of population growth, in either the developed or less developed regions. Moreover, since the rates of output growth have been very similar in both regions over the last 20 years, the correlation is again essentially zero when the two kinds of economies are considered in combination.

What the data show is that population growth has not been sufficient either to force economic stagnation or to dominate empirical comparisons. However, when the specific causal interrelations involved are viewed directly, it appears clear that rapid population growth in the less developed countries has been a decided obstacle rather than an aid to economic growth and that the more rapid the rise in numbers, the greater the deterrent effects.

Urbanization. At subnational levels, such as individual urban or regional areas, the cumulative impacts from population change may work far more rapidly and have much greater relative importance. However, clear-cut demonstration of the welfare and policy implications of subnational population movements has been impeded in the past by other kinds of difficulties. No well-defined order of social priorities surrounds population settlement and distribution. The desirability of reduced versus constant fertility, or of sharper versus more gradual decline, would hardly seem cause for controversy in the less developed countries. However, the merits of slower as against speedier urbanization become murky when their counterpart phenomena of greater as opposed to lesser rural increase are also considered. Excessive urban build-up and agrarian overpopulation tend to be simultaneous phenomena in most less developed countries and no "lesser of two evils" theory has been developed to compare adequately, much less help choose between, the policy options they represent. Nor is there a more encompassing methodology at hand for dealing with entire systems of settlement, in which towns, villages, and secondary-size cities, in addition to rural areas and primary cities, would be evaluated as alternative residences. Some further consideration of this complex of questions is attempted in other sections of this volume.

Macro Gains from Lowered Fertility

The similar output expansion rates in the developed and less developed regions since about 1950, coupled with their very different population growth rates, have produced a persistently widening gap in their average per capita incomes. It is true, and should be emphasized, that the recent rates of per capita product growth in the less developed countries have not been small when viewed historically. However, it is also clear that the continued high fertility in those countries has represented a costly lost opportunity for raising levels of living at rates consistent with remarkably effective productive performance. If the less developed regions could raise their current per capita income growth rates by one third, it would reduce their per capita income doubling time from somewhat over 25 years to 18 years. Under current circumstances this could be accomplished entirely through a fall of the average birth rate in the less developed regions from their roughly 40 per 1,000 level to 30 per 1,000, a 25 percent shift, which, in addition to its income effects, could have perhaps equally large family-welfare effects not captured by conventional income measures.

A larger decline in birth rates, down to the level of the developed regions—less than 20 per 1,000—would raise the stakes commensurately, again quite apart from food crises or other resources-disaster possibilities.

These comparative statistical judgments are, of course, essentially empirical and short-run. Whether they reflect stable long-run causal relations is at least highly problematic (though a number of specific case studies have suggested similar effects from commensurately large shifts in fertility). Much existing theory in this area—for example the classical "laws" of diminishing returns—has been irredeemably qualitative or deductive; practically none, including standard capital-output approaches, has been modeled sufficiently for statistical application and testing. Among the very limited numbers of statistically operational models that have been put forth, there are marked tendencies to utilize essentially the same—though untested—structural relations and to specify key parameters more nearly through crude empirical analogies with developed areas than by direct estimation. Such models probably overstate the influence of demographic factors affecting real savings and investment and understate such relatively "population independent" factors as exports and industrial development programs. Existing theory also understates the role of productive and distributive innovations and changing quality of work force, including the entrepreneurial sectors.

The magnitude of the macro gains to be expected in the low income countries from reduced fertility and slowing population growth over longer periods than a very few decades is probably impossible to determine reliably with present tools of analysis. What is needed are models that are predictively potent, yet can encompass the long lead times required before significant or even visible economic impacts can be traced to altered fertility trends. Assuming, for example, a sudden 25 percent decline in fertility, total personal consumption would not vary greatly in much less than 15 years (especially when the smaller consumption needs of children compared with those of adults are taken into account); educational and related collective consumption needs would stay largely unchanged for the better part of a decade, and neither labor-force size nor numbers of households would be substantially modified for something like 20 years.

Whether fertility in the less developed countries continues at current levels or declines drastically, the expected numbers in the 15 to 65 age group—the main labor-force ages—would be practically unchanged for 15 years and the rate of increase would vary only by about 5 percentage points over 20 years. For the main school-going ages of 5 to 15, a 5 percentage point effect after 10 years compares with one of well over 25 points in 20 years, with very similar orders of effect for total population, hence consumers, over these same time spans.

Persuasive explanatory or predictive models for dealing with demographic-economic interactions during or beyond such prolonged time intervals have not been devised.

In developed areas, fluctuations in fertility, rather than sustained levels or trends, have been predominant determinants of population growth rates during recent decades. The main impacts of such fluctuations often have been upon short-term aggregate demand rather than upon long-term supply. Here too, however, nondemographic factors—for example, employment policy, investment propensities, and foreign trade—have been important enough to command greater attention from policymakers and analysts. As in the less developed countries, the macro-economic effects of demographic trends typically require longer time intervals to acquire sufficient causal significance than do many of the main nondemographic variables.

These comments help explain why attention to "population problems" has been so largely of a "crisis" variety, in both the developed and less developed regions. A further and more serious possibility is that adverse effects of rapid population growth on economic factors are likely to be understated or discounted, as compared to nondemographic factors. Whether or not such impacts are fully discoverable, even in principle, their presumptive longer-run magnitudes and probabilities are nevertheless sufficiently established to accord them a high priority, once the relevant, and distinctive, time spans surrounding their operation are given their due weight.

Research over the past 2 decades on the relations between long-term trends in production and traditional factor inputs (land, labor, and capital) suggests that these factor inputs have accounted for surprisingly small parts of the observed growth in output. After allowances are made for changing amounts of labor and capital (including land), well over half of such increases in output in a number of countries have been identified as "residual," i.e., statistically unexplained. The inference is that other factors, in particular improvements in the quality of the labor force and general technological change, have been the foremost determinants of economic growth in modern industrial history.

This line of reasoning could have important implications for understanding demographic-economic interrelations. It would relegate to a much more secondary position the role of diminishing returns; it would not expect the adverse impact from rapid growth (of both total population and the labor force) to work mainly through adverse shifts in factor proportions (ratios of capital and other nonlabor factors to labor inputs). Adverse effects of rapid population growth are more likely to arise from the impact of growth on the "residual" processes themselves—for example, through significantly reduced opportunities for raising levels of education, health, and other human-resource-developing programs.

Population Growth and Technology

Modern technology has increasingly been directed toward doing better or more cheaply or in a greater variety of ways those things that most people in the poorer countries cannot afford to do at all. A quick review of ten or twenty major innovations of the past 2 or 3 decades will confirm this seemingly sweeping generalization. Thus, until recently much new technology has had only limited relevance to the problems of less developed countries and, in a number of instances, has even affected them adversely. The "Green Revolution" is a recent and major departure.

This does not mean that technology cannot be or has not been imported from the richer countries. Indian steel mills, Brazilian petrochemical plants, and synthetic fertilizer plants around the globe are very important examples. The question is whether rapid population growth has impeded native development, importation, or adaptation of technology. Evidence on this point is scarce, perhaps because traditional analysis has focused on the availability of capital.

It has been argued that in the obverse situation—i.e., relatively scarce labor vis-à-vis land and capital—a pressure for technology develops to substitute for manpower, and that the emergence of technology in the early history of the United States was a response to such a situation. To the extent that this is true, it is a historical circumstance that will not coincide with the special requirements of the less developed countries, because the heavy emphasis on labor-saving in modern technology—including agriculture—does not meet the needs of countries with surplus labor or underemployment.

It can also be argued that there are a number of ways in which population growth has indirectly been a factor in retarding technology, though again evidence is not at hand. First, given the priority of food in the consumer budget, new technology has been most urgently needed in agriculture. The basic scientific principles that could generally be applied have long been available, but, to be successful, new agricultural technology requires the cooperation of a large, widely dispersed, unorganized mass of small producers who must be reached and reoriented. This requires time, programs, policies, organization, division of labor, and a market economy, all of which are scarce in a developing country.

In addition, natural environments differ sufficiently to make straightforward technological transfers in agriculture difficult, if not impossible. Finally, until a few years ago, governments in less developed countries showed little enthusiasm for promoting improvements and investing funds in agricultural productivity. Instead, in an effort to diversify and develop in the image of the industrialized countries, they gave preference to those segments of the economy that are most characteristic of modernity. But the inescapable primacy of agriculture, rooted in the need to feed rapidly growing populations, has been a brake on the progress of industrial technology, native or imported. Neglecting agriculture forced increasing diversion of resources to the importation of food. Both the failure of the governments of developing countries to establish technological priorities that conform to needs and the failure of developed countries to offer attractive alternatives prevented the expected gains of modern technology from materializing.

By holding down per capita income growth, population growth has constrained significant increases in the demand for nonagricultural goods and for services that could more readily have been supplied with the adoption of foreign technology. This consideration must be tempered, however, by the recognition that prevailing low per capita income levels themselves constitute a serious impediment. To rise from a national per capita income of, say, $100 per year to levels that can and do support a large number and variety of goods and services, such as those of the United States or western Europe, would— even at an annual per capita income growth rate of 3 percent—take almost 100 years.

A further adverse circumstance has been that nonagricultural, industrial raw materials (e.g., ores, fuels) from low income countries have been primarily destined for foreign markets. Exported prior to processing, they call mainly for unskilled labor. Low wage rates have kept the need for new technology from becoming a pressing matter. Moreover, these sectors of production in less developed countries have tended to be relatively insulated from the rest of their national economies, so that whatever new production technology develops does not easily spill over into the economy generally, a circumstance that is equally true for the plantation-type, export-oriented segments of agriculture. These "dual economies"—for example, in prewar Indonesia—have been extensively discussed in development literature.

Individuals and Households—Micro Effects

In both developed and less developed areas, demographic analysis has tended to focus on macro or social-scale implications and little on micro effects that occur at individual or household levels. The social costs in individual or household terms of rapid population growth tend to be chronic, even if severe; they are rarely the stuff of public crisis. However, family health and child care—until now considered outside the economic market and nonmonetary in nature—have begun to receive closer attention.

Several workers have hypothesized that there are linkages between fertility levels and the productive (including entrepreneurial) capabilities of the labor force. Family size (or average number of children being cared for simultaneously over a considerable stretch of their pre-adult ages) has been proposed as being causally—and inversely—related to intelligence, child health and care, educational opportunities, and actual school performance. Such effects might be the outcome of two sets of causal factors: reduced "investment" in human resources when family income must be distributed over more children; and possible influences of larger family size as such, with income held constant. Most of the evidence available on the topic bears predominantly on the first class of effects, which, reduced to essentials, are really forms of intergenerational transmission of poverty, a long-familiar subject. Whether family size as such is significant for economic growth is still speculative at best and would probably require at least 10 to 20 years of intensive study to provide reasonably definitive answers, given the inherently longitudinal nature of the transmission processes in question.

However this may be, the processes may have much more significant, as well as visible, implications when the effects of family size are viewed directly in welfare terms, rather than as indirect productive inputs. The effects of rapid childbearing and shortened child spacing on infant nutrition and quality of child care, as well as on maternal health in low income countries, might turn out to be large. Such effects, along with many other "quality of life" indicators, are still largely "beyond GNP." However, even conservative allowance for their existence in benefit-cost terms could yield large income-equivalents. Indeed, given the substantial fraction of the total population annually involved directly with births in the high-fertility areas (perhaps one fifth or more, using a birth rate of 40 per 1,000 and assuming families of five or more including parents), the gains to individuals and families from fertility declines not only would tend to accrue more rapidly, but also might possibly be greater, than the corresponding macro-income effects that can be deduced using more conventional methods of measurement. Merely a one-child reduction in number of children ever born to each mother, if accompanied by commensurately extended intervals of child spacing, would affect the large majority of couples in the reproductive ages, and hence the majority of the total population, within as little as 5 to 10 years.

Socioeconomic Change and Fertility

Finally, a look at the reverse direction of interactions—from social and economic change to fertility—reveals an even scantier base of knowledge. That fertility varies with socioeconomic status has long been documented in

statistical or group terms, but individual or family psychological bases for
fertility have not been amenable to clear definition or successful analysis.
Theories of family decision-making about desired numbers and spacing of
births have all been deductive rather than empirically operational; for
example, they are often developed by analogy with the pure economic theory
of consumer durables.

At macro scales of observation, average fertility differences between highly
developed and distinctly underdeveloped areas regarded as groups–for
example, between nations with per capita incomes of over $1,000 and those
under $400–are among the clearest and most stable comparative phenomena
known to social scientists, but their finer statistical or dynamic structure has
largely eluded analytic approaches. For example, correlations between fertility (birth rates or gross reproduction rates) and standard social and economic indicators have been close to zero as recently as 1960, looking at the
less developed countries as a whole. However, a number of social and non-
income economic indicators (such as communication and education) that
have been examined recently suggest that significant inverse correlations may
hold between these indicators and fertility within individual less developed
regions such as Latin America, east Asia, and possibly others.

To summarize, rapid population growth has neither prevented overall economic growth nor brought about widespread famine. However, rapid population growth has resulted in a slow growth of per capita incomes, per capita
food production, and standards of living while national economic growth
rates are rapidly rising. Moreover, with current population growth rates, the
present optimism about food production need not apply far into the future.
An immediate and continuous decline in fertility would soon increase the
welfare of individuals and households in all economies, and after 15 to 20
years could result in very substantial–and cumulatively rising–overall economic gains, particularly in the developing countries.

POLITICAL AND SOCIAL CONSEQUENCES*

High population density and rapid growth are blamed for many disturbing
features of a changing world: urban violence, political instability, poverty,
pollution, aggressive behavior, revolution, and hypernationalism. Nevertheless, empirical attempts to relate population growth to these political pathol-
ogies have been uniformly unsuccessful. There is no evidence that population
growth decreases the level of political stability or increases the probability of
conflict and violence and aggressive behavior.

* See Myron Weiner, "Political Demography: An Inquiry into the Political Consequences of Population Change," in Vol. II of this study.

One reason for what may be myths about population and political pathology is that population change is ordinarily associated with socioeconomic change, and change carries with it the high likelihood of at least some disruption. Some of the characteristic forms of behavior associated in the public mind with high population density may, in fact, be much more significantly related to the prevalence of poverty and discrimination.

Another reason is the neglect of the subject by serious scholars. In the presence of ignorance, the intellectual gap has been filled by opinion. For example, there is a feeling, quite unsupported by evidence, that people in densely populated countries are more prepared to behave in irrational ways and to seek remedies by violence for internal and external problems, because they value human life less. This feeling is supported sometimes by crude biological analogy and oversimplification of the complexities of the interdependency of demographic and social change.

Nevertheless, the beliefs concerning real or imagined political consequences of demographic behavior are of great political importance in themselves. Hearsay knowledge and ignorance are available to politicians, and, as in the case of *lebensraum*, can be used with great effect to convince people to adopt policies espoused by politicians for entirely other reasons. Clearly the only antidote to unverified hypotheses applied as guides to public policy or as sources of propaganda is to increase the sophistication of tested knowledge and to disseminate the results through public education.

In the following discussion of the political and social consequences of rapid population growth it is essential to bear in mind that the current concern about the negative consequences of this growth are set against the backdrop of powerful pressures to achieve new and higher levels of income, health, education, and well-being. These goals are given differing shades of emphasis depending on the society from which they spring, but it is safe to predict that in the developing countries of the world the great mass of people would happily embrace them all, sure in the knowledge that they need and want more of whatever they are. In an atmosphere of rising expectations political "solutions" have an ineluctable glamour.

Political Administration and Geographic Density

It is difficult to govern a large territory with a small and dispersed population. The high per capita costs of governing underpopulated regions increase the likelihood of conflict between central and subordinate government units when justice, health, and education remain locally based (as is usually the case) because of the difficult problems of transportation and communication associated with attempts by the central government to have continuing contact with the citizenry. This suggests that the larger the population, the more effective its government can be, because the per capita costs of government are reduced. However, difficulties of another kind emerge as density increases. The larger the population, the greater the total cost of government, the less feasible the participation of the individual in the government—except for voting—and the greater the variety of interests seeking to influence the choice among options. With an increase in density, and in economic and social development, the organizational structure necessarily becomes more expensive and more elaborate and the people more subject to regulation, although the increased services government renders may compensate for this aspect.

No matter what the geographic density of people, it is clear that the strains upon the administrative resources of government are increased by the numbers of people that government must serve—just in terms of meeting the increasing demands for public services, such as public security, judicial processes, and legislation. Added to this are the specialized needs such as education, health, housing, transportation, communication, and whatever sort of regulatory devices seem needed to make the system operate with minimum friction. There is a high potential for conflict between central authority located in densely populated urban areas and local authority centered in rural, sparsely settled regions.

Differential Population Growth

Population growth is unlikely to be the same for all parts of a nation's population, partly because the mortality decline that creates growth is likely to be different from one sector of society to another, but principally because growth is ordinarily associated with socioeconomic changes that promote migration from one geographic and/or occupational sphere to another. Population redistribution has major political consequences: the breaking of old ties and forming of new ones on the part of the migrants, the dislocation costs for the sending and receiving populations as well as for the movers, a decline in the importance of systems of local political and social control. As development proceeds, populations tend to concentrate rather than disperse, and regional inequalities tend to become greater. One consequence of this process is that concentration in cities makes political organization more feasible.

Numbers and Political Power. Since numbers constitute an element in the relative political power of social groups, it follows that differential growth rates affect the distribution of political power within a society. This differential may be of less import for social classes than for ethnic groups, since the former are less visible and they gain and lose population by the process of social mobility associated with economic change. Conflicts between ethnic groups, on the other hand, are the counterpart within a nation of the kinds of conflicts between nations—conflicts that may be pursued by means of policies to gain demographic advantage. Ethnic groups are subpopulations with their own patterns of natural increase. Differential size and growth, and the perception of this, are important political facts in all political systems, and perhaps particularly in democratically oriented systems. Population policy may be explicitly or implicitly employed to extend the dominance of one ethnic group over another, or to extend political control over an area not previously well populated, or more generally to influence public policy decisions in discriminatory ways. Intergroup relations may be exacerbated by the migration that generally accompanies population growth and economic development. If low-fertility groups advocate a general policy of low fertility, the policy may be perceived by the targets of the policy to be politically motivated!

From an international viewpoint, political or other social elites may see population growth as a measure of the strength of the nation. Military manpower is still regarded by some as an index of political power despite the lessons of current history. Thus one consequence of rapid population growth may be to stir dreams of political, military, or economic expansionism.

Implications of Changing Age Structure

An outstanding characteristic of a rapidly growing population is the tendency of different age groups to increase at different rates, with the younger ages expanding at a greater rate than the older ages. Conversely, a dampening of the growth rate affects the younger first and only later the older ages. There are three reasons for this pattern of increase by age: The largest decline in mortality is registered in the age group with the highest mortality level, the infants. Second, fertility changes are by definition modifications of the ratio of those aged 0 to those in the childbearing span. Finally, any change at younger ages is passed on with the passage of time to the reproductive ages and is reflected back through the process of reproduction.

A stationary population with high fertility and high mortality is a young population. With mortality decline and the resulting positive rate of growth, the population becomes younger—the more so the higher the rate of growth. When fertility declines, the population becomes older, reaching a maximum age when it becomes stationary at a low mortality level. Thus the typical sequence in a demographic transition is that a young population becomes even younger as a consequence of mortality decline, but then becomes older as a consequence of fertility decline.

This transformation of the age structure has many important ramifications for the body politic. Different age groups make different kinds of demands upon the state—for health services for children and mothers, for the various levels of public education, for employment opportunities for entrants into the labor force, for medical services and social security for the old. For example, with an increase in the number of school-age children, the government may be pressured to divert investment funds from industry to education. More generally, different parts of the social system, to the extent that their membership is age-defined, take on a different relative configuration as a consequence of population growth, and change the power balance of the society. As with the assessment of the consequences of other demographic changes, there are two levels of consideration: a change from a previous equilibrium situation is disburbing to the status quo, and a new stable pattern fails to emerge, so that continual adjustment rather than merely adjustment to a new equilibrium is required.

One outstanding consequence of the modification described is an increase in the dependency ratio as a consequence of an increase in the rate of growth. (The dependency ratio is the ratio of that part of the population unable to produce sufficiently to meet its own needs—say those under age 15 and over 65—to those in the intermediate ages.) Although this is clearly an increased burden on the society, it may be more bearable, because of three associated circumstances: first, the mortality decline that produces the change in the age distribution may be associated with morbidity decline and better health; because the producing population is healthier it is likely to be more productive. Second, the labor force, as the key subpopulation, will, like the general population, be younger. Finally—a more subtle point—it is possible that a decline in mortality, representing as it does a decrease in the role of chance and unpredictability in human affairs, may diminish the sense of fatalism, strengthen the feeling that it is feasible to control the environment and make meaningful long-range plans, promote a sense of future-orientation, and generally increase the prominence of secular rather than sacred attitudes.

One characteristic of a high-mortality society, in toto and within its constituent groups, is a strong correspondence between respect, authority, status, and power, on the one hand, and age, on the other—to some extent irrespective of performance. In a low-mortality, high-fertility society with great numbers of young people, the respect for age and the status quo may sharply decline and those organizations unprepared for this phenomenon may be subjected to great stress.

A final point concerns the possibility that a society will experience change because individual characteristics are a function of age. If, for example, it could be demonstrated that youth is linked with liberalism and age with conservatism, as is commonly believed, then a growing population, because of its more youthful age structure, would be a more liberal population. In apparent support of this proposition, many modern revolutionary movements have been associated with, and have utilized, an increase in the number of young adults. It is difficult to differentiate in this situation the consequences of youthfulness, per se, and the extent to which the brunt of the disadvantages of change falls predominantly on the young adults, or, from another perspective, the extent to which their concentration in urban centers makes them more available for political organization.

In point of fact, little can be said with confidence about the meaning of age for individual behavior in some abstract causal sense, because of two confounding circumstances: (a) Most research on the subject has unavoidably confused its significance as an identifier of the person's location in historical time. Do the political and social attitudes of those over age 70 show the consequence of an inevitable aging process, or are they the result of birth in the 19th century? (b) Behavior in an age is only partly a consequence of the characteristics the individual brings into the situation. Societies are organized to expect particular kinds of behavior, and are ordinarily successful in bringing performance into line with those expectations. One of the most likely accompaniments of a process of social and economic development is a modification of age norms.

Some Special Political Problems

Although the evidence is indeed thin, there is reason to speculate that rapid population growth contributes to (but does not create) certain unique types of politico-legal problems in less developed countries. For example, it appears reasonable to inquire about the size of the bureaucracy as a tool of administrative management in those countries in which there are pressures on the government caused by underemployment and unemployment.

Rapid population growth in rural areas can place remarkable strains on a legal system that presents real or perceived barriers to economic well-being; for example, the way land is held, its passage from generation to generation, and inheritance laws—all influence political decisions. Here the mix of political and economic consequences becomes blurred, and it is abundantly clear that not enough is known about the ways people react to and perceive these problems.

Finally, there is one clear political consequence of rapid population growth that has deliberately been excluded from this analysis: the sometimes exciting politics of fertility control—or family planning. This would be the subject of another entire volume, to say the least. It is possible to expect that education, information, and understanding of the consequences of rapid population growth will in the near future substantially decrease the volatility of this issue in most countries. Nonetheless, a different frame of reference and method of analysis would be required to make any definitive statements on this subject.

Society and the Family

The consequences of rapid population growth for the family depend heavily upon the associated changes that may be occurring in the society and the economy. For example, the arithmetic of child dependency would be very much altered if the society were to prescribe child education and proscribe child labor. Both developments would institutionalize the rights of

individuals, specifically the new generation, over the claims of family obligation, specifically to the older generation, and modify drastically the familism
that has been so congenial to high fertility. Occupational opportunities outside the family farm would be another blow to the parent-child relationship,
particularly since most such opportunities require migration of the child and
allegiances to extra-familial organizations. Such changes would bring into
question the pattern of traditional obligations of children to parents and
place particular strain on the pivotal parental generation, which feel bound
by the traditional demands of their parents without any compensating claims
on their children.

In summary, the new demographic situation of mortality decline and rapid
growth may represent a severe structural strain on relationships within the
family. From one standpoint this situation may be viewed as a grave consequence of population growth; from another standpoint it may be regarded as
a necessary step in transforming the social structure in order to make the new
equilibrium one of low fertility and mortality. The obstacles to such a new
equilibrium are considerable, because of likely opposition from those with a
vested interest in the traditional structure—from some heads of governments,
of armies, of religions, and of families, and from certain of the privileged and
the property-owning. The outcome is obviously problematic, and will differ
in detail from one culture to another, but it seems unlikely that the tide of
social transformation that is sweeping the world can be more than postponed,
whatever the current strength of tradition in any particular society.

URBANIZATION*

Urbanization is a product of a country's history, an irreversible process,
and an inevitable concomitant of economic development. Two thousand
years from now it is possible that our century will be recalled as that time in
history when the population of the world was converted from primarily rural
to primarily urban. Whereas in 1900 probably no more than a quarter of the
world's population lived in urban settlements, by 2000 it is possible that 60
percent or more will be found in cities.

Recent Changes in Rural/Urban Population

The world figure, of course, does not reveal the great range to be found
today. Table 3 provides relevant data on both the level of urbanization and
the tempo of change in the period 1950-70. The developing regions ranged
from a low of 10 percent urban (eastern Africa) to 53 percent (middle
America and tropical South America). Stated generally, Africa south of the

*See Harley L. Browning, "Migrant Selectivity and the Growth of Large Cities in
Developing Countries," in Vol. II of this study.

Sahara as of 1970 had so low a level of urbanization that its period of major transformation still lies ahead of it; at the other extreme, Latin America already has nearly half its population in urban places; and the great populations of Asia are intermediate. If we take 70 percent as the standard for developed regions (excluding Oceania), then by the end of this century only Latin America has a chance of reaching this level, but Asia and Africa may be close to 50 percent.

The same pattern is seen when the city (a place of 100,000 or over) population is examined. (See Table 3.) The relative positions of Latin America, Asia, and Africa are the same.

It is characteristic of the urbanization process that, the more it progresses, the more significant the part represented by large urban places among the total urban population. Even now the developing world contains many of the world's largest urban centers. Shanghai, São Paulo, Peking, Mexico City, Calcutta, and Rio de Janeiro all have estimated 1970 populations of over 7 million. By 2000 the world's largest urban agglomeration will very probably be in a now-developing country.

Table 3 does not show the rate of growth of the population as a whole nor the absolute sizes of urban populations. In Africa for the period 1950-1970 the percentage increase of the urban population was 177; for Latin America, 136; for Asia, 135. By contrast, in Europe the gain in urban percentage was only 39, even though the proportionate increase was slightly higher than for Africa. The explanation is, of course, that Africa had a much higher rate of total population growth. It is also due to the rate of change of the rural populations. In the developed regions of the world, from 1960 to 1970 the rural population declined in absolute terms; in a number of developing regions rural growth exceeded 2 percent per annum.

Since the rate of urbanization in a country can vary only between the known limits of 0 and 100 percent, in the life span of any given country the period of intense urbanization during which the society is transformed from a primarily rural to a primarily urban one occupies a comparatively short time span. The peculiar problems that are associated with rapid urbanization are not permanent features in the history of a society. It is this feature of urbanization that gives a sense of urgency to efforts to affect and to guide the urbanization process. Many developing countries are now in the most critical period, and others are now on the threshold, of this transformation.

The Tempo of Urbanization

Urbanization is always the product of a unique historical development. Once the pattern is laid down it is usually very difficult to alter. Once begun, urbanization goes forward; a country becomes progressively more urban. (The few exceptions to this rule involve the breakdown of the social order, as

TABLE 3

Levels and Change in the Urban Population
by World Regions, 1950-1970

(percent)

World Region	Urban Population 1950	Urban Population 1970[a]	Rural/ Urban Change 1950-70	Point Difference 1950-70	Population in Cities[b] 1970[a]	Rural Population per Annum Change 1960-70
DEVELOPING REGIONS						
Northern Africa	24.6	34.6	41	10.0	23.1	1.8
Western Africa	11.6	19.7	70	8.1	7.4	2.5
Eastern Africa	5.6	9.9	80	4.3	4.9	2.5
Middle and southern Africa	6.6	15.4	133	8.8	6.0	1.5
Middle America	39.2	53.0	35	13.8	20.1	2.3
Caribbean	35.2	42.5	21	7.3	20.7	1.7
Tropical South America	35.8	53.1	48	17.3	32.2	1.1
East Asia	12.1	25.3	109	13.2	16.1	.3
Southeast Asia	13.6	20.1	48	6.5	12.1	2.3
Southwest Asia	24.2	35.5	47	11.3	21.7	1.6
South Central Asia	15.2	17.8	17	2.6	9.8	2.2
Oceania	4.9	8.5	73	3.6	0.0	2.3
DEVELOPED REGIONS						
Northern America	63.8	75.1	18	11.3	57.4	-.6
Temperate South America	59.1	70.2	19	11.1	52.1	.3
Northern Europe	69.5	74.9	8	5.4	58.2	-.3
Western Europe	63.2	73.0	16	9.8	45.0	-.6
Eastern Europe	42.4	54.6	29	12.2	24.3	-.6
Southern Europe	41.5	50.7	22	9.2	29.6	-.1

[a]Estimated.

[b]100,000 or over.

Source: Kingsley Davis, *World Urbanization 1950-1970. Vol. 1: Basic Data for Cities, Countries, and Regions.* Population Monograph Series, No. 4. Berkeley: Institute of International Studies, 1969.

occurred in the ancient world.) The *tempo* of urbanization is, however, another matter; it varies from nation to nation and from one historical era to another. In general, countries that experienced their most intense period of urbanization in the 19th and early 20th centuries did so at a slower pace than are the developing countries now in their most dynamic phase of economic change. Another difference is, of course, the much more rapid overall population growth in the developing countries of today.

The Green Revolution and Urbanization. The speed of urbanization can be affected by many factors—wars, droughts, revolutions, depressions, booms, for example. It is often difficult to foresee over a decade or so what will influence this speed. The Green Revolution provides an illustration of this point. A transformation only recently begun, it has not spread to all developing countries, and its long-term success is still problematical; yet the Green Revolution promises to have a considerable impact upon the volume of rural-urban migration and therefore upon the rate of urbanization. Because it is based upon technological innovation, primarily the use of fertilizers, the Green Revolution favors the larger, more modern, and commercially oriented farms. This development, in conjunction with high rates of population increase in rural areas, can be expected to increase out-migration to urban areas. (Whether there will be mass migration of whole families and of all ages or simply an intensified exodus of the traditionally migration-prone group—the young adults—is not clear.)

In addition to its possible effect upon the size and composition of migration streams, the Green Revolution may affect future levels of urbanization, because the growing urban population can be provisioned better from internal sources. Higher agricultural productivity makes possible a higher level of urbanization.

Migration—the Major Mechanism of Urbanization

There are various combinations of fertility, mortality, and migration that can cause the rapid growth of urban populations. But it is most common in time and space that the major contributor is rural-urban migration.

To understand the urbanization process in a given region, it is important to know how many people are moving from one place to another. Data on migration streams are indispensable. It is equally important, however, to know *who* is migrating. Demographic characteristics (age, sex, marital status, etc.) and socioeconomic characteristics (education, occupation, etc.) are needed to understand the impact of migration on both communities of origin (rural and urban) and the urban communities of destination. All these factors affect incorporation of migrants into the urban milieu.

Return migration is another aspect of internal migration that is best understood by reference to community of origin and of destination. Reliable information on its magnitude is generally lacking, but it represents a significant proportion of all migrations. To an extent still not determined, return migration acts as a sorting mechanism, returning the less successful and least satisfied migrants back to their communities of origin.

The effect of in-migration on the further growth of urban population depends upon the reproductive behavior of the migrants, a complex phenomenon as yet not well understood. Urban life with its constraints on housing and its system of rewarding the best-trained workers, should encourage small-family norms. Furthermore, the sex imbalance that characterizes much rural-urban migration, the greater knowledge and availability of contraceptives, and a greater incentive to use them tend to lower urban fertility. However, many of the migrants to urban areas are in the prime reproductive period, and there may be a relaxation of traditional constraints upon fertility.

The Absortion of Manpower into the Urban Labor Force

An inevitable consequence of rapid population growth is the virtually universal problem of absorbing natives and migrants into the labor force of cities. Many are never really "absorbed"; they are either unemployed or underemployed. At present there is very little evidence about how much variation in such categories is to be found among countries or among cities within a particular country. And, of course, the problem of absorption into the urban labor force can never be separated from conditions in rural areas from whence the migrants come.

It is pretty well established, however, that the structural transformation of the labor force is accomplished mainly by inter- rather than intra-generational changes: most men do not make radical changes within their work lives; instead, successive cohorts enter into higher-level occupations. Linked to this is the fact that the migrants' success in finding good (stable) jobs in the city is related to their age at arrival in the urban area. If they come at an early age, they are able to compete quite successfully with the natives. Consequently, special importance attaches to the age of entry of men moving into the urban labor market.

The Urban System

The concept of urbanization includes the system of cities—the forms of interdependence among the cities and their relations to hinterlands. Basically, systems of cities are described in terms of the urban hierarchy (the size distribution of cities within an area and the activities, or functions, associated with size) and the spatial arrangement of urban places in terms of their interrelationships with each other and their respective hinterlands.

The distribution of urban places by size in a country is independent of the level of urbanization. In some countries the urban population is concentrated in smaller cities; in others large cities dominate. Although there is no theory that can tell us what urban size distribution is most appropriate for various stages of economic development, several factors may be relevant.

Cities of different sizes generally perform different kinds of functions. The biggest cities in a country are "diversified"; they do not specialize in one kind of activity, such as manufacturing or commerce. Some studies in advanced countries have tried to work out thresholds for various activities that appear only when cities attain a certain population. Unfortunately, there are few if any comparable studies of developing countries, but it seems certain that the results obtained in developed countries cannot automatically be applied to cities in developing countries. Almost certainly, the threshold for the appearance of many activities will be higher in contemporary developing countries.

An independent but related problem is determining economies and diseconomies of scale of different city sizes. Few would argue that there is a direct relationship between size and overall efficiency. At some point the diseconomies stemming from high land rents, traffic congestion, pollution, etc. will come to balance out or outweigh the advantages of population concentration and high division of labor. So little hard evidence is available on this point that little can be said other than to note that differences between developed and developing countries may be considerable.

These considerations come to a head in dealing with one prominent feature of the urban hierarchy, the position and role of the "primary" or first city of a country. Many developing countries are characterized by "high primacy"; the first city is many times larger than the secondary cities, and this demographic concentration reflects a high degree of concentration of governmental, economic, and cultural activities in one place in the country. There has been a tendency to condemn all cases of high primacy as being detrimental to economic development because they are "parasitic"—sucking out the best from the rest of the country and offering little in return.

However, conditions vary among countries. As an example, two countries may demonstrate equally high primacy; their first cities are five times the size of the second cities. In one country a review of the situation leads to a recommendation that the pattern be maintained, whereas in the other country the recommendation is to use all means to reduce it. Why the contrary policies? The first country is small in population (say 5 million) and compact in area. Assuming a good transportation network, the primary city is within a few hours of all populated parts of the country. The advantage of maintaining high primacy and moving, in effect, toward a city-state pattern is that it will permit the existence of at least one genuinely metropolitan center that can provide the range of goods and services that a modern country requires. One city of a million inhabitants may be better suited to the country's needs than five cities of 200,000 each. The other country has 50 million people and encompasses a large irregular area; therefore high primacy may handicap regional development. The one center cannot well serve such a large and dispersed population. And the primary city would attain so large a population that it would result in local diseconomies. In short, in primacy variation just as in other aspects of urbanization, no simple formula will suffice.

The Spatial Position of Cities and Regional Development. Regional planning is now accepted in principle in most developing societies. What is still not common, however, is an explicit recognition of the part that urbanization, and in particular the spatial location of urban places, could play in the elaboration of regional plans. Frequently, regions are defined—as, for example, river-basin authorities—without any reference either to the existing urban structure or to what it might become. The fact that cities are nodal points in the process of development is lost sight of. The role they play as "central places" in providing goods and services to an agricultural hinterland or to some lower level of urban places too often is neglected.

Within most developing countries there are areas that can be termed, from an urban standpoint, undeveloped (very low degree of urbanization and poor internal and external communiction); underdeveloped (substantial urbanization but not well articulated with the resources of the region); and overdeveloped (too much urban concentration—primary cities are the most striking example—in relation to resources such as water). Each of these situations requires its own set of directives. In particular, regions classified as undeveloped need careful attention, for it is here that the urban regional planner can do more than try to correct earlier mistakes. He can be instrumental in laying down an economically and socially viable network.

Costs and Benefits of Urbanization

At the beginning of this section we stated that urbanization is an inevitable concomitant of economic development. Yet much current discussion suggests that urban centers are a handicap to development, as shown by such terms as "overurbanization," "pathological urbanization," "parasitic cities." Whatever the merit of these criticisms, it should be remembered that both historically and currently a close relationship—that has been frequently demonstrated statistically—exists between indices of economic development and indices of urbanization. In the most general terms, productivity is greater in urban than in rural environments, because, briefly stated, the concentration of population brought about by urbanization permits a higher division of labor and reduces costs caused by the "friction of space."

There is great uncertainty about how to interpret studies that have tried to estimate the monetary cost of urbanization, i.e., how much money is needed to create a new job for a rural-urban migrant. The results usually show such high costs that it is concluded that it is better to reduce rural-urban migration drastically and to make efforts to keep prospective migrants in their rural communities of origin. It is difficult to argue with the arithmetic of these studies, but it can be asked if they are attuned to the reality of the situation. Any similar study in the period of intense urbanization of now developed countries would probably have yielded the same conclusions. Housing, for example, is and always has been a particularly troublesome problem for societies experiencing rapid urbanization. It is doubtful that any country (possibly a Scandinavian one might be an exception) has been able to provide "satisfactory" housing, be it England in the 19th century, the United States at the turn of the century, or the Soviet Union following the Revolution. Some of the standards that are used in making the calculation of urban services have been unthinkingly imported from the developed countries of today. In Latin America, at least, there now seems to be a better appreciation of both the desire and ability of squatters and low income groups to improve their housing substantially through self-help measures.

Surely one reason why more attention seems to be drawn to the ills of the city is that they are much more visible and concentrated than they are in the country. Since they are linked to the amount of documentation or observation, reports of worse conditions in the cities are, in most cases, statistical artifacts.

For example, in developing countries, nearly all cities have a mass of unemployed and underemployed workers, but underutilization of manpower is a characteristic of both urban and rural sectors. Education and health services are often more available in urban areas.

Urbanization does have its own set of "costs," and the form that the urbanization pattern takes may not be well suited to the requirements of a country. However, major policy issues would still arise if urbanization were to be perfectly "proportioned" relative to economic development. Criticism of the degree of urbanization and the speed of the process is often misdirected; policy changes should be directed to the systems of cities within a region—the problems rooted in the urban size hierarchy and the spatial distribution of cities. The question is not whether urbanization is desirable—it is probably inevitable—but what form it should take.

EDUCATION AND POPULATION GROWTH*

There is considerable evidence from recent economic research that factors other than the amount of capital investment in the means of production or growth in the quantity of labor are of major importance in economic growth. Such growth requires much more than an accumulation of capital and an increase in the number of workers. New types of productive instruments have to be created, new occupations generated and learned in new contexts and locations, new types of risks have to assumed, and new social and economic relationships have to be forged.

Hence, the development factors include: (a) improvement in the quality of labor through education and other means of skill acquisition, as well as better health and welfare; (b) more favorable conditions for the introduction of

*See the chapters in Vol. II of this study by Gavin W. Jones, T. Paul Schultz, and Harvey Leibenstein.

innovation and technical change; (c) institutional changes leading to more effective organization and management at both governmental and private levels; and (d) a better environment for entrepreneurs. These factors are interrelated, and all depend to some extent on improvements in education.

Recent Educational Expansion

The number of children enrolled in the primary schools of the less developed countries rose 150 percent during the 15 years from 1950 to 1965, and the percentage of all children 6 to 12 years old who were in school rose from less than 40 percent to more than 60 percent. This marked increase in enrollment ratios (the fraction of the total age group who are in school) reflected in large measure the value placed on education by people of all classes and income groups in the developing countries.

Public pressure for more education probably came in part from increasing economic returns to skill and education as industrialization proceeded and in part from the widening disparity between the incomes of people who had some formal education and those who were illiterate. This disparity in turn came from the growing demand for skilled labor and the stagnation in demand for uneducated and unskilled workers, whose numbers were rapidly increasing because of high rates of population growth. Studies in four Latin American countries and in India show that the earnings of people with 5 to 6 years of schooling are double or triple those of persons who have spent less than 2 years in school. Persons with 11 years of education earn three to six times as much as functional illiterates.

Education of Children as a Form of Saving and Investment

Educational expansion means that many parents have been spending more to improve the education and skills of children even though this has become more difficult as the number of children in each family increased. These investments in the "quality" of children may be taking place at the expense of savings by households and corresponding capital investment in the physical means of production. Statistical analysis of a large number of less developed countries shows that the level of savings measured in terms of national income remains, over time, a relatively constant fraction of per capita incomes. This fraction does not increase as per capita incomes rise, but from country to country it shows a strong inverse correlation with child dependency ratios, that is, the proportion of children less than 15 years old to adults 15 to 65 years old.* (As we have seen, these dependency ratios depend directly on

*Nathaniel H. Leff, "Dependency Rates and Savings Rates," *Amer Econ R*, Vol. 59, No. 5, Dec. 1969. pp. 886-896.

birth rates and rates of population growth.) Total savings, including those invested in human capital through education and better nutrition and child care, though still low in absolute terms because of low per capita incomes, are considerably higher than monetary savings or investments in physical capital and may be rising more rapidly than per capita incomes.

Limitations on Expenditures for Education and Development

Allocating expenditures for education presents difficulties on the government, as well as the family, level. In low income countries public investments in education reduce the amount that can be spent by governments on capital investments for short-term increases in production. The proportion of the gross national product (GNP) that can be drained off in taxes by all levels of government is limited by the necessities of human survival. In India, for example, 60 to 90 percent of personal incomes must be used to meet the physiological needs of the people for calories, protein and other nutrients, clothing, and shelter. Governments also face other difficulties in raising sufficient direct and indirect taxes to provide the revenue that must be shared among education, health and welfare services, and capital expenditures for development. These difficulties arise from the low levels of exports and imports available for customs revenue and the frequently deteriorating terms of trade, the prevalence of family morality rather than public morality, and the lack of effective political and economic controls.

The situation of average households in low income countries is similar to that of governments. There are difficulties even when per capita incomes rise. The ratio of total savings to income cannot be increased very rapidly as per capita incomes grow, even if strong incentives exist, simply because the necessities of life require that a high proportion of income be used for food, clothing, and shelter. Increasing numbers of children in the average family keep this proportion high even when total family income rises. In economic terms, the "elasticity" of savings to rising incomes tends to be close to one. This means that consumption needs are not adequately met by present income and the bulk of any increase in per capita income will be used for increasing consumption rather than savings.

Educational Costs per Child in Developed
and Less Developed Countries

On the average the developed countries with their high per capita incomes are able to spend both a greater percentage of national income and far greater amounts of money on public education than the poor countries. This contrast is widened by the large proportion of children in the developing countries, a result of high birth rates and low death rates. Therefore, even if the level of educational expenditure were the same, expenditures per child would be much less than for low-fertility countries. For example, in 1965 the United Kingdom used 6 percent of its GNP for education, while Ghana used 5 percent. But the school-age population (5 to 19 years) was about 37 percent of the total population in Ghana and 22 percent in the United Kingdom. Thus Britain used nearly twice as large a percentage of its GNP per head of the school-age population as did Ghana. In absolute terms, the United Kingdom, with a GNP per capita of $1,800, spent about $500 per child for education, and Ghana, out of a total GNP per capita of $300, spent $15 per capita, or about $40 per child.

Education in the developing countries is further handicapped by the fact that educational costs per child in schools, in terms of per capita incomes, tend to be relatively high. The differential in incomes between educated and uneducated people is much larger than in the developed countries, and consequently the ratio of teachers' salaries (which constitute 60 to 80 percent of educational costs) to per capita incomes is commonly two or three times this ratio in developed countries.

Percent of National Income That Can Be Devoted to Education

The low incomes of developing countries are not in themselves a fixed barrier to the channeling of substantial proportions of income into education, provided governments give education a sufficiently high priority and are able to raise the necessary taxes. There is a wide variation among countries, but on the average they spend about 3.5 percent of national income on education. But there does not appear to be much correlation between per capita GNP and the percentage of national income devoted to education. At all levels of per capita GNP, this percentage varies widely, from 1.5 to 2 percent in Ethiopia, Pakistan, Nicaragua, and Portugal to about 6 percent in Kenya, Ivory Coast, Cuba, and Libya, and more than 8 percent in Zambia and Tunisia. Expenditures per child of school age have an even greater range, from less than $5 to more than $75.

Future Increases in Enrollment Ratios

In spite of the rapid expansion of education in the less developed countries, the absolute numbers of illiterates in these countries increased from 1950 to 1965 because of the population factor; the number of children in the primary age group rose more rapidly than the number being educated. Educational planners in Africa, Asia, and Latin America are aiming at a reversal of this situation in the future by raising enrollment ratios to above 90 percent as rapidly as possible.

Time Required to Raise Enrollment Ratios. In many countries such an increase in enrollment ratios would be extremely difficult and perhaps impossible to accomplish in less than 15 to 20 years. One reason is that accelerating rates of population growth and the low levels of secondary and higher education during the past 2 decades have resulted in a small proportion of potential teachers relative to the numbers of potential students. Teachers must be recruited from the smaller and more poorly educated cohorts of these past years, in some regions in the face of competition from industry and other sectors. Moreover, the increase in the percentage of the GNP used for education that is required to raise enrollment ratios can be attained only rather slowly in many countries, because it requires a reorganization of fiscal and tax procedures that may not be possible until the GNP becomes much larger than at present.

Savings in Enrollments Resulting from Reductions in Fertility. If the desired rise in enrollment ratios takes place over 20 years or more, the rate of growth of the school-age population will greatly affect the total numbers of children in school. This can be seen by analyzing the situation of a typical developing country in which the population of children 5 to 14 years old is increasing by 3 percent per year, and educational plans call for a rise in enrollment ratios from 40 percent at present to 95 percent after 20 years. If fertility remains constant over these 2 decades, the number of children in school at the end of the period will have increased by 338 percent. With a steady decline in fertility at a rate of 1.7 percent per year the increase will be 270 percent. If fertility declines by 3.3 percent per year for 15 years, the numbers of children in school will have increased only 206 percent. Thus the savings in enrollments resulting from sharply reduced fertility will be about 30 percent after 20 years. The effect after the first 10 years would be much smaller however—about 3 percent—because of the 5- to 6-year lag in the effect of a reduction in fertility rates on school-age population.

If the rise in enrollment ratios from 40 percent to 95 percent takes place over 30 years, the constant fertility projection gives a 517 percent rise in enrollment at the end of this period, whereas for a rapidly declining fertility the increase would be only 200 percent. A 51 percent saving in enrollment would be attained at the end of this period by the assumed rapid reduction in fertility. Fertility reduction would give a saving of only 3 percent at the end of the first 10 years, and 30 percent at the end of 20 years, just as in the previous case.

Effects of Declining Fertility on Costs of Education. The effects on future educational costs of declining fertility rates versus continuance of present high fertility are more difficult to visualize than the effect on future enrollments. A rise in enrollment ratios with continuing high fertility will require that an increasing percentage of GNP be devoted to education, even if GNP increases more rapidly than population. This results from the fact that the costs of education per student increase about as rapidly as per capita incomes. Most of these costs represent teachers' salaries, and these rise as per capita incomes rise.

Moreover, if the school system is to be expanded and improved, the proportion of expenditures for buildings and equipment and the nonteacher component of recurrent costs must be raised. To create a more balanced system the ratio of students in secondary and higher education, relative to those in primary school, must be increased, even to ensure a sufficient number of primary teachers. In Africa and Asia, secondary education is six to fifteen times more expensive per student than primary education, and university education twenty-three to thirty-nine times more. Finally, improvement in the quality of education must be attained primarily through raising teacher qualifications, and this means both greater costs and a lengthening of the time for teacher education, and a rise in salaries more than proportional to the increase in per capita incomes, if education has to compete for personnel with industry and other sectors.

For a given increase of GNP, per capita incomes will be higher if fertility declines and population growth is slowed. Hence the cost of education per student will increase more than if fertility had remained constant. Consequently, the effect of a fertility decline on educational costs will be less than proportional to the reduction in the number of children to be educated. But calculations for a typical case—Pakistan—show that whether or not enrollment ratios and educational quality are improved, total educational costs would be significantly smaller if present fertility rates were rapidly lowered than if fertility were constant. This is basically due to the fact that the proportion of children to adults in the population would diminish. In 1985 the percent of GNP required if fertility remained high would exceed that required for rapidly declining fertility by 13.9 percent if enrollment ratios held constant, by 10.4 percent if enrollment ratios are raised, and by 9.4 percent if, in addition, pupil/teacher ratios are lowered. In 1995, the excess in the high-fertility case would be 38.5 percent, 29.9 percent, and 27.5 percent respectively. By 1995, the amount saved each year would be about 900 million dollars, more than four times the *total* expenditures for education in Pakistan in 1970.

High Rate of Economic Growth Required to Increase Enrollment Ratios. The calculation for Pakistan assumes a growth in GNP of 6 percent per year, or about 350 percent by 1995. Even with this very high rate of growth, more than 8 percent of national income would have to be devoted to education in order to accomplish the planned increase in enrollment ratios, unless there is a marked decline in fertility. Practically no country today allocates such a high percentage of resources to education. If the economy grows at a slower rate, the increase in enrollment ratios would probably be impossible to attain without a sharp reduction in fertility.

Urbanization and Education

Another consequence of high rates of population growth that affects education is the rapid urbanization that is occurring in most less developed countries because of migration of redundant workers and their families from the countryside. Both enrollment ratios and educational standards are usually higher in urban than in rural areas. Therefore, educational planners need to keep these differences in mind and to take into account the rates of urban migration both in planning the allocation of educational resources and in budgeting additional funds for raising enrollment ratios and improving educational quality.

Allocation of Educational Resources

Without greatly increased educational expenditures, the necessity of providing primary education for rapidly growing numbers of children inevitably diverts resources away from technical, vocational, and higher education, all of which are required in many countries to provide the skilled technical manpower essential for economic growth. One of the most difficult problems faced by educational planners and administrators is to strike an optimum balance between the two kinds of education, in the face of public pressures for expanding school enrollment ratios and for a broader geographic distribution of schools.

The Role of Education in Reducing Fertility

The quantity and quality of education affect fertility rates, and hence population growth, in several ways:

1. Education postpones the age of marriage. Educational opportunities for women, particularly secondary and vocational education, tend to raise the age of marriage. This is clearly seen in the Khanna District of the Punjab in northwestern India, where the age of marriage of women has risen from less than 17 to more than 20 during the past decade as education and employment in teaching, nursing, and other occupations have become available. This postponement of marriage is one of the contributing causes to the decline of the birth rate from 38 per 1,000 in 1957-59 to 32 per 1,000 in 1966-68.

2. Educated women have fewer children. Evidence from several countries shows that women with 7 or more years of schooling have fewer children and smaller families than women who have had little or no education. The reasons are complex and not entirely understood, but among them are probably the greater access to information and to communications media possessed by educated women; the alternatives to childbearing available to them in the form of jobs and opportunities for service; their increased role in family decision-making; their greater ability to provide adequate nutrition and better health for their children, with the result that they are faced with less uncer-

tainty about their children's survival; and their realization that a small family will make it easier to provide education and social mobility for the children.

3. Educational costs to the parents lead to smaller desired family size. Even when the costs of teacher salaries and the capital and equipment costs of education are paid by the state, children in school are a considerable expense to their parents. Their material needs are greater and they are less able to contribute to family income. Hence parents perceive their interests are better served by having fewer children.

4. Economic and social development resulting from education tends toward a reduction in fertility. As we have pointed out, an increase in the quality and skills of the labor force, together with other individual and social characteristics related to education, are probably the most important elements in economic and social development. At the same time, there is evidence that a certain level, or rate, and character of development are necessary conditions for a marked decline in fertility under the present circumstances of less developed countries. Although both these propositions rest largely on statistical grounds and are difficult to quantify or state in any rigorous fashion, the empirical relationships seem clear. We may say with some conviction that an increase in the quantity, an improvement in the quality, and a raising of the average level of education in most developing countries would promote economic development and thus a slowing down of population growth.

Time Lags in Educational and Economic Development

Both high rates of population growth and the poverty that is synonymous with underdevelopment severely impede a rapid expansion of education. The time lags for interaction between population and economic change and educational improvement are long. A reduction in fertility would significantly improve educational prospects only after about 10 years; there is also a lag of about 10 years in the effects of education on economic development and on fertility. Neither the developed nor the less developed countries can afford to relax their efforts to bring about a reduction in fertility by all acceptable means or to take advantage of every opportunity for capital investment and institutional change that offers a possibility of speeding up the development process.

CONSEQUENCES FOR PUBLIC HEALTH AND HEALTH SERVICES*

Public health technology applied on a mass scale in the developing countries has reduced death rates dramatically. Yet the level of personal health

*See the following chapters in Vol. II of this study: John Cassel, "Health Consequences of Population Density and Crowding"; Leslie Corsa, "Consequences of Popula-

services for the individual and the community varies widely and, in general, remains far below the levels of the more developed regions. National leaders and the public aspire to a level of health services that will reduce mortality still further and increase the health and well-being of the people. However, as with education and other public services, high fertility forces health ministries to run fast to stay in the same place—let alone improve services. Unlike other services, however, personal health services can have a direct effect upon population growth by reducing mortality and by providing family planning services.

Governmental health expenditures in most developing countries are between 0.3 and 2.5 percent of GNP, ranging from less than 30 cents to several dollars per person per year. In most developed countries these expenditures are between $13 and about $75 per person and the fraction of GNP is usually between 1 and 4 percent.

Population Growth and Personal Health Services

For the next 20 years at least, the demand for health services will outrun the supply—by any measure such as doctor/population ratios or number of hospital beds. Rapidly growing population combined with higher aspirations make this inevitable. A study of doctor manpower needs from 1955 to 1965 in thirty-one developing countries illustrates the problem of numbers.* To maintain the doctor/population ratios of 1955, 25 percent more doctors were needed because of rapid population growth. To increase the doctor/population ratio by 3.3 physicians per 100,000 people, from 17.9 to 21.1, 50 percent more doctors were needed by the end of the 10-year period. At zero population growth, only 18.5 percent more doctors would have been needed.

The age and geographical distribution of the population also affects the health services. In a high-fertility community the primary stress on health services will be the care of mothers and children. The problems of medical treatment for infants are substantially greater than the problems of treating young adults, and hence care of the young requires a higher doctor/population ratio than the care of people aged 15 to 45. The levels of personal health services are usually much higher in urban areas than in rural ones, both in terms of numbers of physicians per capita and in facilities.

In a high-fertility region many women have several pregnancies very early in their childbearing years and continue to bear children up to the time of menopause. Very young mothers, older mothers, mothers with closely spaced

tion Growth for Health Services in Less Developed Countries—An Initial Appraisal"; and Abdel R. Omran, "Abortion in the Demographic Transition."

*World Health Statistics Report, Vol. 21, No. 11, Geneva, 1969.

pregnancies—all high-parity mothers—face risks. Except in most favored socio-economic groups, evidence suggests that a short interval between pregnancies depletes the mother's capacity to give her baby a good start. She also carries a higher risk for her own health and safety, especially if she has several pregnancies very early in her childbearing years. Fetal loss rate under such circumstances is higher, infant survival is lower, and malnutrition and some impairment of growth and development are found in the surviving children. Mothers not only suffer from illnesses associated with pregnancy and childbearing, but are more vulnerable to other health hazards of a more general nature. They bear the burden of caring for the children, often under unfavorable circumstances and frequently with fewer opportunities to avail themselves of any health services that may exist.

With closely spaced pregnancies, or high parity, or the combination thereof, there is also greater risk of early interruption of pregnancy and of prematurity. Where breast feeding is the only chance a child has to survive, early birth of another infant curtails the benefit from the mother's lactation and predisposes the child to Kwashiorkor or other types of malnutrition. Studies from the United States and the developing countries reveal the not surprising fact that, as family size increases, per capita spending for food goes down. As a result, corresponding diet inadequacies and nutritional deficits are common. Malnutrition in childhood is usually not clearly identified in mortality statistics, for it is largely reflected in deaths from dysentery, measles, pneumonia, etc. to which undernourished children have lessened resistance.

Abortion

Rapid population growth is usually paralleled by a lack of community experience in the use of contraceptives. The result is a large number of unwanted pregnancies, and, in many countries, frequent resort to induced abortion, particularly when the desirability and feasibility of limiting family size become recognized.

Abortion is widely considered both a social and a medical (or health service) problem. The sociocultural aspects of this problem are so varied and so intimately associated with the historical, legal, and religious patterns of individual countries that it is difficult to attempt any brief analysis of their complexity or to generalize about the way rapid population growth affects specific situations. It is possible, however, to assemble an impressive amount of evidence to give weight to two generalizations about abortion.

First, it appears that as traditional societies (no matter where) begin to make the transition from high to low fertility, the popularity of induced abortion as a method of fertility control rises markedly. It may even reach what has been termed epidemic proportions in some societies. Second, lawmaking bodies are becoming increasingly convinced by the argument that the costs and dangers of illegal and unskilled abortions outweigh whatever other arguments are advanced in behalf of restrictive abortion laws. Arguments for community health and safety, and for women's personal freedom, are carrying the day in many communities, although the acceptance of legal abortion is far from uniform from one society to another or within societies.

To the health planner this situation presents some very serious questions, whether abortion is a legal or extra-legal means of fertility control. The prevalence of induced abortion beyond the law (particularly if in epidemic proportions) results in serious demands on health services for medical salvage procedures. In some hospitals in developing areas, from one fourth to one third of hospital maternity beds are used for postabortion cases. Yet low-cost legal abortion service cannot be provided unless there is a realistic resource base of facilities and trained personnel. This must be one element in the decision whether to provide legal abortion facilities as a major component of a fertility control program designed to contribute to social and economic development. Insofar as possible, the need for abortion should be minimized by providing women who wish to avoid pregnancy with easy access to contraceptive materials and information.

However, the complete elimination of abortion through the effective use of contraceptives is a distant and probably not attainable goal. In those societies in which the drive to limit family size is strong, the use of abortion tends to rise. It also tends to rise after the inception of effective and extensive contraception programs which help to inculcate a small-family norm. Nonetheless, experience in Japan and the USSR shows that the goal of eventually decreasing the rate of induced abortion by the use of other family planning methods is feasible when accompanied by intensive education and information programs.

Family Planning

The leaders of many developing countries see high natality levels as a handicap to overall development. During the next 20 years the trend toward expanded and intensified family planning programs will undoubtedly increase. In some societies, there are already attempts to achieve specific lower levels of population growth. In others the emphasis is more general—to improve maternal and child health and to alleviate the poverty that is associated with large families.

A national family planning program and government health services can interact in three ways:

(1) Particularly where a variety of fertility-control methods is offered, and especially if these include sterilization or abortion, the family planning program will often be a part of the personal health services provided by the government. The requirements for frontline workers are different for some

kinds of family planning programs than for other health services; the program management should have a high and semi-autonomous status; and the costs should be considered as new and additional to those for other services.

(2) If a drop in birth rates results from the family planning program, the need for personal health services will be less than it would be with continuing high fertility. For example, in a country in which the level of health services is being doubled, a 25 percent decline in average rate of population growth would produce a 15 percent saving in annual health expenditures at the end of 20 years, compared to the expenditures required if the rate of population growth is unchanged. The effect on maternal and child health services will be proportional to the decline in birth rates and will be felt as soon as a decline occurs.

(3) The family planning program may compete with the personal health services for scarce medical facilities and personnel, including physicians and trained nurses. Where family planning programs and health services are combined, there may also be a direct competition for funds; the budget for an effective family planning program is likely to be at least half the health services budget in those developing countries that spend less than 1 percent of GNP on health. Competition for personnel, facilities, and funds will arise as soon as the family planning program is initiated, before it has had an appreciable effect on fertility. The extra demand for physicians can be minimized by employing family planning workers who are not physicians, but who have been especially trained to carry out the necessary physical examinations and other activities required in the family planning program. This has been tried successfully in Pakistan. Modern techniques for induced abortion greatly reduce the time requirements for physicians to perform abortions, and the number of days spent in hospitals by abortion patients.

Health Consequences of Density and Crowding

The commonly held view that crowding and population density, per se, have deleterious effects on health probably derives largely from four empirical observations: (a) Traditionally the densely populated (i.e., urban) areas have *reported* higher death and morbidity rates. (b) Industrialization and urbanization have frequently been followed by dramatic increases in death rates attributable to infectious diseases. (c) Studies of military training camps have reported exceptionally high rates of virus diseases. (d) In some laboratory studies, deleterious health consequences are noted as the number of animals housed together is increased.

The orthodox explanation for these observations is that crowding increases infectious disease, mainly through a greater opportunity for the spread of infection. For example, outbreaks of upper respiratory infection among recruits in military training camps are explained as the result of the herding together of large numbers of susceptible young men with a few infected individuals. But there is evidence that crowding also has other injurious health effects, which occur primarily during the period when the degree and extent of crowding is rapidly increasing. The effects appear to be much less serious when the rate of crowding is slow and the crowded population has sufficient time to become adapted to its environment.

Thus rapid population growth and its accompanying rapid urbanization are probably more injurious to health than actual population density. In many cases, however, it is difficult to isolate the effects of crowding, as such, from other conditions, such as poverty, poor nutrition, poor housing, and pollution, which formerly characterized all cities and still prevail in the rapidly growing cities of the poor countries, and in the "inner cities" of the United States.

Before the modern era, cities were often called "eaters of men"—their birth rates were usually lower than their death rates, and the population was maintained by continuing migration from the countryside. Even as late as 1950, urban death rates in the United States were slightly higher than rural ones. But by 1960 the situation had reversed, and in 1966 death rates in cities and towns were only half as high as those in rural areas. The incidence of infectious illness was much lower. This was at least partly the result of better sanitation and health facilities in the cities and suburban towns, relative to the rural areas, plus the fact that migration of younger people to the cities had left an older, more susceptible population behind in the countryside. Low morbidity and mortality also characterize crowded areas in other countries with high levels of health services and sanitation. For example, although Hong Kong and Holland have very high population densities, they are said to enjoy two of the highest levels of physical and mental health in the world. The levels of mortality and morbidity in the densely populated cities and towns of Great Britain are about the same as those in rural areas.

Both animal experiments and experience with human beings indicate that social stresses due to crowding produce physiological disturbances. In turn, these increase susceptibility to both infectious and noninfectious disease. The effects are most severe before individuals have had time to become adapted to the crowded conditions. In animals, physiological changes occur during the period when the size of the population in the same space, that is, the population density, is increasing. These changes include increased adrenal and other endocrine secretions and a higher level of activation of the central nervous system. It is believed that they result from increased social interactions which enhance emotional involvement and produce excessive sensory stimuli. Animals in subordinate positions within the group tend to respond in a far more extreme fashion than those at the top of the social hierarchy, both in the volume of endocrine secretions and in manifestations of disease and pathology. After the population has reached its maximum size and has become adapted to the crowded conditions, the level of physical pathology drops to that of animals living in an uncrowded environment.

Some of the ameliorating effects of urban adaptation in human beings are suggested by the death rates from lung cancer in the United States. When controlled for the degree of cigarette smoking, these death rates are considerably higher in farm-born people who have migrated to cities than in life-long city dwellers. In a study of Appalachian mountaineers working in an urban factory, it was discovered that the first generation suffered from a high rate of illness and absenteeism; their sons did not.

In the rapidly growing cities of developing countries, the newcomers can be expected to be at the highest risk for another reason as well. A frequent accompaniment to urbanization is the atomization or destruction of the family and kinship groups that provide protection and emotional support to rural individuals. In the course of time, new types of groups develop in the cities to fulfill some of these functions, but it is often difficult, particularly for newcomers, to become effectively integrated into these groups. Individuals who are deprived of such meaningful group relationships, exposed to ambiguous and conflicting demands for which they have had no previous experiences, and frustrated at achieving their goals and aspirations, may be more likely to become victims of both infectious and noninfectious disease. Insofar as this effect exists, it is difficult to distinguish from the direct consequences of a rapid increase in the level of urban crowding.

It should be evident from this discussion that the magnitude and nature of the effects of crowding on human beings are highly uncertain. Much research is needed to clarify and quantify them.

Consequences for Children*

Many studies have been made of the effects of family size on the well-being of children within the family. In families with many children there are more malnutrition and illness of children than in small families; higher mortality rates among younger children; slower physical growth; and less intellectual development. Family size is not the only cause of these effects, but it is probably an important element in the interacting network of causes.

Excessive "crowding" of children, especially in a family with a young mother, seems to produce the same effects as excessive numbers of children. That is, the effects of short spacing between births are about the same as those of large numbers of children in the family.

---

* See Joe D. Wray, "Population Pressure on Families: Family Size and Child Spacing," in Vol. II of this study.

Infant and Child Mortality Related to Family Size, Birth Interval

In less developed countries infant and child mortality is much higher in large families than in small ones. For example, in eleven villages of the Indian Punjab during 1955-58, 206 out of 1,000 children died during the first year of life in families in which the mother had given birth to seven or more living children. In families of only two children, the infant mortality was 116 out of 1,000. The difference in mortality rates was even larger for children between 1 and 2 years of age—95 per 1,000 for the children in families of seven or more live births and 16 per 1,000 for two-child families. The same proportionate differences in mortality rates between children of small and large families are found in New York City, though the levels of mortality are very much lower.

The effects of short birth intervals on infant and child mortality in low income families are painfully illustrated by data from these Punjabi villages. In 1955–58, 310 out of 1,000 children, born less than a year after a preceding child, died during the first 2 years of life. This mortality rate was 55 percent greater than that of children born between 3 and 4 years after a previous birth, and more than twice as high as the mortality rate among children born after an interval of more than 4 years. The proportional differences in deaths during the second year of life between the three groups of children were about twice as large as the differences during the first year, though the mortality rates were considerably lower.

Family Size and Physical Development

In low income countries the high mortality rates among children in large families, and in families with close birth intervals, are in part due to malnutrition. The greater the sibling number, the greater the likelihood of malnutrition among poor families. Studies of preschool children in Colombia, for example, show that 52 percent of the children in families in which there were five or more preschool children were seriously malnourished, whereas only 34 percent of children in families with only one preschool child were malnourished. In Thailand, of the children whose next youngest sibling was born within 24 months, 70 percent were malnourished; of those in families without a younger sibling, only 37 percent.

Since growth is related to nutrition, it would be expected that the height and weight of children in large families would be smaller on the average than in small families. Even in high income countries the children of poor families are larger at any given age when the number of children in the family is small. For example, of 2,169 London day school students 11.25 years old, children from one-child families were about 3 percent taller and 17 to 18 percent heavier than children from families with five or more children.

The difference in physical growth between children of small and large families in Great Britain seems to affect mainly the poorer social classes. In the higher income classes boys in families with three or more children are taller at all ages than boys in small families; the reverse is true for girls. In the upper and lower manual working classes children in small families average 3-4 percent taller than those in large families at 7 and 11 years of age, and 1.4 to 2.8 percent taller at 15 years.

Effects on Intelligence and Educational Performance

Large numbers of children in the family diminish not only physical size but also linguistic skills, intelligence as measured by intelligence tests, and educational performance. These elements are to some extent interrelated; for example, heavier children mature earlier, and early maturers do better in school than late maturers. Experiments show that the apathy that is a major consequence of malnutrition is highly correlated with such psychological elements as lack of ambition, low self-discipline, low mental alertness, and inability to concentrate.

Both physical growth and the greater cultural nurture associated with small families appear to affect intelligence. In the sample of British day school children, intelligence increased with height and decreased with family size. The average verbal reasoning scores of children over 135 centimeters tall in families of one or two children were 5 to 7.5 percent higher than those of children of the same height in families of four or more children. The difference for children of the same age but less than 135 centimeters tall between large and small families averaged about 7 percent. Tall children from both large and small families scored about 6 percent higher than short children.

In studies of Scottish children the average I.Q. of only children was 113, that of children with five or more siblings was 91. In France, only children between the ages of 6 and 12 had an average mental age 1 to 2 years higher than children with eight or more siblings.

The differences in educational performance between children in small and large families are especially significant when the families are separated by social class. Data from the British National Survey of Health and Development show the performance of children in families of different size in educational tests at 8 and 11 years of age. In the upper manual working class, only children and those in two-child families scored about 11 percent higher than children in families of six and about 26 percent higher than children in families of seven or more children. The difference in the lower manual working classes between only children and children in large families was about 17 percent. In the upper middle class the difference in educational performance between children in large and small families was somewhat less than 9 percent. The difference in educational performance in all classes was slightly larger at 11 years than at 8.

A study in Scotland found the negative correlation between intelligence test scores and number of siblings held true for all social classes. In France, it was "clearly apparent" for children of farmers and manual workers, but "barely discernible" for children of the professional classes.

That the difference in children of large and small families persists in adult life is indicated by the average scores of army recruits on tests of different types in Great Britain. In the tests that measured general, verbal, and special mechanical intelligence, the recruits from small families scored 11 to 16 percent higher than those from families with five or more children, and the difference increased with increasing family size. On the other hand the difference in tests of physical ability was much smaller, only about 5 percent.

Possible Reasons for Greater Intelligence in Children of Small Families. It is likely that the ability to think abstractly, which underlies most kinds of human problem-solving, develops at an earlier age and to a greater degree if children learn the necessary verbal skills either from adults or from siblings considerably older than themselves. The smaller the family size, the easier it will be for children to develop such skills. These concepts receive support from psychological evidence that suggests that a young child's intelligence level can be raised by the environment in which he is brought up, including the cultural stimuli provided by the family, or by an urban setting. A high proportion of persons of outstanding intellectual achievement were either only children or came from families in which there was a large age gap between siblings.

Children in large families may suffer more maternal deprivation because of greater maternal illness and the stress of large numbers of children on the mother. The effects of extreme maternal deprivation are drastic and impressive. They result in lower linguistic skills and I.Q. scores and less success in later life. In one study, 50 percent of children deprived of maternal care were in a state of dazed stupor—apathetic, silent and sad, making no attempt to make contact with others, often suffering from insomnia, prone to infection, and dropping behind other children in development. The effect of extreme maternal deprivation is also well shown by comparing children brought up in institutions with those brought up in foster homes from early infancy. At the age of 3 years the I.Q.'s of the institutionalized children were 28 points lower than those of the children who had been cared for by foster parents.

An important question remains unanswered: Would the parents of large families among the poor have provided better for their children if they had had fewer of them, and would the children, in consequence, have achieved greater physical and intellectual development? Parents who *do* limit family size may be qualitatively different from those who do not. If the difference exists, it might result in both smaller numbers of children *and* healthier, more intelligent children in some families than in others. Alternatively, parents who *do not* limit family size may have the same potential as those who do, but because they lack knowledge of, or access to, means of limiting family size, they are unable to do so, with the result that, *because* of excessive family size, their children are subject to more illness, receive less adequate nutrition, fail to grow well, and do not achieve their full potential for intellectual development.

These two alternatives are not mutually exclusive. The first may apply to some parents, the second to others. As we have seen, there is evidence that most parents in the less developed countries would like to control their family size. Many of them have more living children than they wanted to have. For those parents to whom the second alternative applies, the number of children they wanted might have been better cared for if the ones they did not want had not been born. If effective means were made available for all parents who want to control their family size to do so, a considerable proportion might use these means, and be better parents as a consequence.

Importance of Intelligence for Development. Intellectual capacity and the ability to manipulate abstractions that typify educated intelligence are important to economic development not only through the contribution of skilled specialists, such as engineers, lawyers, physicians, architects, and teachers, but also because of the broad category of managerial skills, from farm budgeting to central administration, that rest on intellectual capacity and the greater ability of intelligent workers to adapt to change and innovation.

Environment and the Quality of Life*

The assertion that rapid population growth adversely affects man's environment and the quality of life itself is rarely challenged. In developed areas we see the sky above the city veiled in thick smog, mining scars in mountainsides, dying lakes, rivers discolored from industrial effluents, billboards along highways, conversations interrupted by overpowering noises from passing jet planes, spots of scenic beauty marred by accumulations of empty containers and transistor radio chatter—an incomplete list that increases year after year; in less developed areas—wildlife displaced by artificial lakes, new irrigation canals spreading schistosomiasis to previously uninfected areas, land that should not be cultivated denuded and eroded, and native populations uprooted. Although each encounter with these environmental insults seems renewed evidence that the quality of life is indeed deteriorating, a number of questions must be asked about the role of population growth.

*See Joseph L. Fisher and Neal Potter, "The Effects of Population Growth on Resource Adequacy and Quality," in Vol. II of this study.

Population–Only One Variable

First, population growth is only one of several variables that affect the quality of life, however defined. Per capita income, the state of technology, the degree of concentration of human settlements, and the social and cultural diversity of the population are others. There is little doubt that, at least in the developed countries, sheer numbers are not nearly as important in causing pollution as are the high levels of consumption and the by-products of a highly developed and diversified technology. As pointed out in the section dealing with resources, the rise in energy consumption, for example, is due far more to increases in per capita income than to the growth of population, and many adverse effects can be attributed to technical factors that are not inevitable concomitants of energy production and consumption. Thus it would be a gross oversimplification to blame numbers of people alone for the set of problems confronting modern society. Moreover, it is impossible to isolate the effects of a single variable–like population–and picture life in a world adjusted for a different value of that variable unless we allow for inescapably associated changes in other variables. We may shed tears for the adversities or insults that confront us, especially as we compare them with our private visions of what might have been or could be, but we can never know what tears we might have shed had different combinations of factors given us a different world.

Preferences and Costs

For example, in the United States or western Europe the relatively low price of owning and operating private automobiles, closely associated with the rise of a mass market due to a large population and high incomes, has been a prime factor in making faraway places accessible, but the same automobiles in urban areas produce noxious gases that now befoul the air beyond the air's capacity to dilute or transport them. What is the net effect on the quality of life? Where is the trade-off between newly won mobility and clean air? Would the benefits of overcoming the adverse by-product, through new technology or through the modification of economic incentives, or both, be sufficiently attractive to stimulate manufacturers and users to pay the costs of developing and using products that do not befoul the air?

The point is that our reactions tend to be lopsided. In a way, the interest rate by which we discount the future also operates in looking back, but unevenly. The ugliness, dangers, and adversities of the past (called "the good old times") are heavily discounted in comparison with those of the present. Evaluating "trends" becomes a matter of impressions, difficult if not impossible to define in some objective fashion. Thus we are driven to look for more reliable indicators, such as conditions of the environment, natural and man-made, that we can measure, albeit with difficulty.

Yet a new difficulty arises. The question of what constitutes "the good life" is as old as man. What is new is that, for much of man's existence, it has been up to him, within limits, to elect to lead the good life. Today we question the quality of life, because it is perceived that deterioration is *imposed* upon us, since it operates on the environment in which we live.

To be sure, people do not *prefer* polluted rivers and air or *demand* jet noises or billboards as conditions of their continuing happiness. Indeed, these decisions do not ordinarily confront them. When they contract to buy a good or service, the price does not include the portion usually referred to as "social costs," i.e., costs that are imposed on society as a whole, or a given part of it, such as degradation of river water, of air, of a tract of landscape, etc. The market fails to let all who are affected participate. Participators include, beyond the buyer and the seller, others living and people yet unborn, whose lives will be affected by choices made now. The market reflects only a slice, albeit a large one, of the interests and costs involved. By excluding the social costs, it leaves them to be dealt with by different means, if at all. When they appear in a context that requires citizens to make a decision to forego other advantages and perhaps to pay directly, there is evidence that the associated price tag tends to lower the priority of the necessary remedial action. People will complain vigorously about the garbage that accumulates in public places, including those of scenic beauty, and will demand remedial action; but until they begin to perceive the ecological damage they suffer, they tend to resist more than nominal charges to alleviate the situation. Under these circumstances, the pocketbook is a fair indicator of these preferences, and that indicator throws doubt on the intensity with which people deplore various well-known blights—even in these times of deep concern about the environment. If social costs were included in the price of goods and services, those with high social costs would be less in demand and the shift in consumption patterns would lead to an enhancement of environment.

Some observers contend that preferences revealed in market behavior are not reliable guides to perception; instead, people act in certain ways because either (a) they have no option to act differently (that is, they go to crowded places because they do not have the means to go to those that are less crowded), or (b) they are uninformed or ignorant of ways to act that would lead them to treasure those aspects of life that are being appreciated by the "sensitive few," and give proper weight to societal problems. That is, were it not for market failure and insufficient information, people's preferences would reveal greater concern for quality.

Actually, little is known about preferences—how many prefer, say, rubbing shoulders as opposed to the number seeking solitude. Moreover, relevant research would have to take account of the fact that solitude, beauty, and similar intangibles are obtainable only at a cost, and a rising one. It is quite possible that a generation born and raised under conditions of crowding will not object to, and in fact may feel more comfortable in, crowds.

In developed countries the upper and middle income groups take material advantages for granted and are acutely conscious of the secondary effects these advantages produce. In the same societies the lower income groups are far more conscious of their material needs and tend to ignore side effects.

Measuring Changes in Quality of Life

Measuring changes in the quality of life should take account of both improvements and deteriorations. It should be a *weighted* average taking account of differences in preferences and reactions at specified levels of cost, and perhaps of intensities of such preferences (which surely would have a very real effect in a market situation).

It is one thing to judge that things are "bad" and quite another to judge that they are "worse." As has been suggested, there is little evidence on the second, especially as one looks further and further back and is careful to add up the pluses and minuses. There is, on the other hand, widening and justified attention to how "bad" matters are in terms of quality.

Partial answers can be obtained by considering deterioration of specific *aspects* of life. Although good measurements still are scarce, air pollution, water pollution, urban density, overcrowding of recreation areas, etc., as evidenced in recent years, suggest a worsening. To the best of our knowledge, these conditions have not as yet become irreversible (except for vanished species); that is, they are, at a cost, amenable to treatment by both new technology and changes in incentives and institutions. It is perhaps worth noting, however, that the one area probably least amenable to such treatment is deterioration in the "space-solitude-privacy" complex due to sheer rise in numbers of people (from the subway rush to the crowded recreation spot), a phenomenon to which there is as yet no promising approach. This statement is not contradicted by the likelihood that life in a metropolis can provide more social privacy than in a small town. There are a few well-developed devices for dealing with the "overload" of environmental stress caused by numbers and proximity. But the intrusions, especially those of a physical kind, become harder to ward off, notwithstanding adaptive behavior. And they surely are a factor in the quality of life.

Problems in Low Income Countries

Most of what has just been described applies more to high income than to low income countries, partly because living at the margin of subsistence in developing countries allows little to be finally disposed of or abandoned, i.e., the rate of recycling is high. Low income restricts both the magnitude and the variety of consumption, including consumption of energy in all its manifestations. The ills caused by poverty leave little room for concern about—or expenditures for—the environment in ways that now preoccupy many people in high income countries.

The kinds of environmental adversity that exist for the less developed countries result much more from rapid population growth combined with a *lack* of technology than from rising incomes and the *presence* of new technology. In agricultural areas, extension of cropping into rain-fed areas that are at best suitable only for grazing, and of grazing into areas that should not even be grazed—prevalent over much of the arid Middle East, for example— has led to extremely poor soil conditions, remediable in part by better management (e.g., controlled grazing) and new technology (scientific farming).

> Many of the savannah or semi-desert areas . . . are the worst abused land resources and the resulting erosion presents a major problem requiring not only technical solutions but legal and social regulation of grazing use, a very difficult task to enforce in nomadic or semi-nomadic communities.*

Rapidly rising population aggravates this kind of resource pressure, as well as the pressure caused by a lack of cheap fuel, leading in many places to near-total gathering as fuel wood of any shrublike vegetation that might otherwise begin to take hold.

Large new engineering structures, especially dams and lakes, although permitting increased production also bring their share of ecological problems. Extension of waterborne diseases, of undesirable plant life (e.g., water hyacinths that clog water courses, transpire water to the atmosphere, etc.) are well known. The need for heavy fertilization and application of pesticides that are inescapable accompaniments of a Green Revolution set in motion other disturbances, some of limited spatial extent, some having more far-reaching consequences. The very rapid spread of new technology designed to feed rising populations may have secondary effects on the environment to a degree and an extent yet unknown. Worldwide alertness to these dangers in developing countries may provide the time and the incentive for timely countermeasures.

Many of the primary environmental problems of the high income countries, correlated with a high degree of industrialization, mechanized transport, and high fuel use, have not yet appeared in poorer countries and are not likely to show up for some time, given low income levels. Here again, the experience of the richer countries could provide useful indicators of impending trouble.

Finally certain environmental phenomena could, if continued, threaten the survival of man. They derive basically from alterations in certain ecological systems, brought about by man-made interference. Modifications in the heat balance of the earth, ocean pollution, effects of radioactive waste emission in air or water, and genetic mutations triggered by chemicals are a few examples

*U.N. Food and Agriculture Organization, *Provisional Indicative World Plan for Agricultural Development*, Vol. 1., c69/4 Rome, August 1969. p. 45.

of such contingent threats. Unfortunately, these threats are poorly understood, and the degree to which they are mounting is uncertain since we generally lack reliable "baseline" data. Usually several variables are involved, working in different directions, and the degree of certainty with which we can predict both future trends and effects is small. Neither panic nor complacency is an appropriate response to this situation. These contingencies deserve the most careful investigation and monitoring, particularly in the developed countries today, because here even a very small probability of a very serious result should give rise to remedial action. Continued rapid population growth certainly will aggravate the effect of the unwisely applied technology or faulty economic incentives that have produced their emergence.

IV

Population Policy

In a sense, all the policies of a nation that involve the welfare of the nation's people are population policies, but we are concerned here with policies related to changes in the quantity and quality of the population and its geographical distribution—in the numbers of human beings, their education and skills, and where and how they live relative to the space and resources available to each person.

As we have shown, the rate of change of population size, the levels of fertility and mortality, the distribution of people between urban and rural environments, and the rate of change of this distribution significantly interact with the social and economic welfare of people.

TWO KINDS OF POPULATION-RELATED POLICIES: POPULATION-RESPONSIVE AND POPULATION-INFLUENCING

The governments of nearly all countries are committed to improving the welfare of their peoples, and population-related policies are one of the tools available to them for this purpose. Present rates of population growth are so high in most less developed countries that two kinds of policies are called for: *population-responsive policies* that will ameliorate or overcome the effects of unprecedented increases in population size and density, high birth rates, and high population growth rates; and *population-influencing policies* that will bring about a reduction in fertility and mortality and in growth rates, or will beneficially influence internal migration. Policies concerning employment, food supply, building of cities and towns, and resource development are in the first category; family planning programs and other policies to reduce fertility, public health and nutrition programs that lower mortality, and transportation and industrial planning to influence internal migration are in the second.

In much of the following discussion, we shall concentrate on *population-influencing policies* aimed at fertility reduction. We recognize that in several developing countries with large land areas, relatively sparse populations, and high fertility rates, government leaders may consider the need for a larger

70

population so pressing that they may be willing to forego the economic and social benefits of reducing fertility. We urge that in these nations the leaders (a) make themselves thoroughly aware of the demographic dynamics of their country and its interrelations with economic and social development, and give adequate attention to population growth and change in formulating development policies; and (b) examine closely the extent to which the substantial penalties to development that result from high fertility and rapid population growth and the benefits of reduced fertility and slower rates of growth may apply in the special circumstances of their country now and in the next 2 or 3 decades. Even a marked reduction in rates of population growth to the levels suggested later in this chapter will result in a doubling of population size in less than 50 years.

Asymmetries in Population Policy

There is a considerable asymmetry in the possible range of population policies for less developed countries. Policies to accelerate mortality declines are feasible and may be desirable, but on both humanitarian and political grounds no option exists either to increase mortality or to abandon efforts for further mortality reduction. Policies to reduce fertility are feasible and desirable, but policies to increase fertility significantly are not feasible because birth rates are already at a high level. Internal migration from the countryside to towns and cities is widespread in developing countries and may be subject to modification by policy, but except for certain special situations such as emigration from islands with limited resources, and emigration to alleviate political or ethnic conflicts, sustained international migration on a sufficiently large scale is neither politically feasible nor economically reasonable as a solution to population problems. Though greater freedom of international migration throughout the world is desirable from many points of view, it cannot now contribute very much to alleviating the effects of population growth, because the size of the earth's population is now increasing so rapidly.

The total number of people who emigrated from Europe and Asia to North and South America and Oceania during the 19th and early 20th centuries was about 60 million. This is less than 1 year's increase in the world's population at the present time. Transocean air and water transportation facilities have become very much greater during the past 50 years, and the aircraft and ships now exist to move this large number of people across the oceans each year. But even with enormous capital investments for education, job creation, housing, and other social infrastructures, it would probably be impossible for present sparsely populated countries to assimilate in their existing economies and societies the number of migrants required to offset significantly the problems of population growth in more crowded countries.

The needed teachers, managers, construction facilities, and institutions simply do not exist. Without such assimilation, population problems would in no way be ameliorated; they would simply be transferred geographically. Moreover, immigration is almost always differential; the young men, the able, and the venturesome would be the first to migrate, and those who were left behind in the home country would suffer grievously from their loss. A transfer of a much smaller amount of capital than that required for immigrant assimilation from the presently rich countries to the poor ones would probably go much further in bringing about economic and social development of the poor countries, and thereby in creating the conditions for a marked reduction in fertility and the rate of world population growth.

More than a thousand million hectares of arable but uncultivated land exist in North and South America and Africa. The longer the time during which world population continues to increase, the more likely it becomes that there will be no economic alternative to making very large capital investments to bring these areas under cultivation and to settle them with large numbers of people. But for the foreseeable future, food supplies can be increased to match human food needs much less expensively by raising yields and by multiple-cropping on presently cultivated land. Capital for agricultural development will be better spent and new technology more effectively applied on the farms of India and Pakistan, where almost all arable land is already cultivated, than in the sparsely settled parts of countries in which there are large areas of uncultivated arable land.

POPULATION-RESPONSIVE POLICIES CALLED FOR BY HIGH RATES OF FERTILITY AND POPULATION GROWTH

Rates of population growth in less developed countries are at least half, and in some cases almost equal, the rates of economic growth. Chiefly because of the high fertility of these countries, the ratios of children to adults are also very high when compared with these ratios in developed countries, and both the numbers of children and of young people entering the age of labor force participation are rapidly increasing. Because of these factors, planners and political leaders should take future population growth and change into account in all long-range planning. The following are a few examples.

Health and Educational Manpower

The numbers of teachers, physicians, and health workers who need to be trained must be equal to the sum of replacements for those who retire or die, plus additional personnel to keep up with the growing numbers of children in school and the numbers of children and adults requiring health services. If the absolute number of functional illiterates (with less than 5 years of schooling) is not to increase, school enrollment ratios must rise, and, hence, the number of teachers to be trained must grow faster than the growth in population. This will also be true of physicians and health workers if the number of people for whom health services are unavailable is to be lowered. One task of policymakers in health and education is to balance the demands for quantitative increases due to population growth against the needs for improving the quality and level of education and the distribution, range, and effectiveness of health services.

Food and Agricultural Production

During the 1950's, development strategies in many less developed nations were concentrated on attempts at industrialization, in part based on the example of such recently developed countries as the Soviet Union. But these strategies did not reckon with the unexpected and unprecedentedly high rates of population growth which appeared after World War II and accelerated throughout the next 15 years. Though industrialization sometimes proceeded at a rapid pace, industrial employment usually increased more slowly, and the absolute number of people supported by the industrial sector lagged behind the growth of population, with the result that the number of people tied to the land in agriculture greatly increased. At the same time, population growth has brought about a vast increase in food requirements. Consequently, agriculture continues to be the base of the economy in most of the less developed world. In recent years, it has been widely recognized that much greater emphasis on agricultural improvement is essential for overall economic and social growth, and more balanced development strategies have been undertaken.

In Asia, where nearly all arable land is already farmed and most of the world's people live, a revolution in agricultural technology must occur if rapidly growing populations are to be fed even at present levels, let alone improved diets. For both economic and physiologic reasons, the rate of growth of food supplies should be substantially greater than the rate of population growth. The situation is summed up by the FAO.*

Assuming a 2.6 percent annual increase in population there will be an extra one billion people in the developing countries by 1985. This alone would require an 80 percent increase in food supplies by that year compared with 1962, without any improvement in quantity or quality of individual diets. Success in raising income levels along the lines proposed in the "high variant" of the economic model, and consequent improvements in purchasing power, would increase demand for food by 142 percent

*U.N. Food and Agricultural Organization, *Indicative Plan for Agricultural Development, Main Conclusions and Policy Indications of Provisional Indicative World Plan.* Rome, August 1969. Vol. III, p. 57.

above the 1962 level, an average rate of increase of 3.9 percent per year. As against this the trend in food production over the decade 1956-66 for the developing countries taken as a whole was only 2.7 percent per year.

Agricultural revolution has already begun with the introduction of new high-yielding, fertilizer-responsive varieties of wheat, rice, and other cereals. If it is to continue, large expenditures for development of irrigation water, transportation, storage, food processing, and fertilizers must be made, including large amounts of imports requiring foreign currency. This will require overall economic development at a higher rate than has recently prevailed. These demands must be taken into account in planning resource allocations and priorities, and in raising capital funds.

The new agricultural technology is much better suited to some regions than to others. In India, irrigation development is easy to accomplish in the Gangetic plain of Uttar Pradesh and Bihar; it is difficult and expensive in most of the Deccan plateau, which covers central India. In East Pakistan, existing new cereal varieties cannot be grown and chemical fertilizers cannot be used, except for one crop during the dry season, in the 30 percent of the country that is flooded for 5 months each year. National farm prices will almost certainly fall because of greatly expanded production in the regions in which the new technology can be successfully applied. The farmers in the less favored regions may then be unable to sell their crops at prices sufficient to pay for the water, chemical fertilizers, and other inputs needed for high-productivity agriculture. They will be forced back on subsistence farming, but this will be insufficient to feed the growing populations of their own villages. Large numbers of poverty-stricken and unskilled countrymen will be driven out, either to cities and towns or to the more favored agricultural regions, where most of them will become landless laborers. The challenge to policy-makers, either to develop new agricultural technologies for nonirrigated land, or to provide employment and a new way of life for these people, is very great, especially because of the difficulties, already alluded to, of raising employment in the industrial sector as fast as the labor force grows.

In the regions in which the new agricultural technology can be successfully applied, capital and land give greater returns than labor, and, hence, it can be expected that the larger landowning farmers will gradually take over from the smaller ones and from tenants. This situation will increase still further the proportion of landless laborers and will aggravate inequities in income distribution. New land-tenure policies or other means to protect small farm-owners and tenants are called for. Problems of unemployment and underemployment may be increased as a result of unchecked agricultural mechanization, unless labor-intensive agriculture, combined with selective mechanization that increases the demand for labor, is strongly encouraged by the governments (e.g., tubewells to provide irrigation water and cultivating machinery for rapid seedbed preparation, which will facilitate growing an extra crop during the year).

Rapid population growth in rural areas in which the supply of arable land is limited results either in a fragmentation of farms from one generation to the next, or in an enforced migration of younger sons and their families to towns and cities. The average size of farms in the Punjab of West Pakistan has decreased by about 50 percent in one generation. The effects of farm fragmentation can be overcome by the formation of agricultural cooperatives among the small farmers, but experience in less developed countries shows that this usually occurs only under the impetus of strong government or outside encouragement.

Urbanization

In most less developed countries, cities are growing more rapidly than total populations, at least partly because stagnant rural economies have not been able to absorb rural population growth. In one carefully studied region of the Punjab in northwestern India, the rate of emigration during the 1950's equaled half the rate of natural increase of population. The situation has been considerably improved during the last few years by the rural prosperity resulting from the agricultural revolution described earlier. But in other regions, such as East Pakistan, where rural population densities average more than 1,200 people per square mile, the labor/land ratio cannot be much increased even with the multiple-cropping and increased crop yields brought about by the new technology. With present rates of population growth in the Province, room must be found in cities and towns during the next 20 years for some 15 million people. It may be impossible to accommodate these numbers in existing cities, and if so, new cities and towns and new industries must be created on a very large scale. Planners and policymakers will have hard choices to make in dividing scarce resources between investments to provide industrial and service jobs, and construction of housing, roads, water supply and sewage disposal systems, and other elements of urban infrastructure. Much experimental research needs to be done on lowering these costs of urban development. Other choices must be made between developing many small cities and towns of ten to fifty thousand inhabitants or large cities with millions of people. These choices should be based on a careful analysis of the full range of social and economic costs and benefits of each kind of urban place, the functions that can be filled by towns and those that must be reserved for cities, and the possibilities of influencing migrant behavior. One advantage of having many urban centers is that people may continue to live in the country and commute to a nearby city or town for employment. Thus, the small cities of Comilla in East Pakistan and Ludhiana in the Indian Punjab draw many villagers for daytime employment who return on bicycles and buses to their rural homes at night.

The lot of rural migrants to the cities of less developed countries would be greatly improved if they received more information about urban job opportunities and living conditions and training for city life before emigrating, and a more supportive reception when they first arrive in the city. Educational curricula, information media, and institutions need to be developed for this purpose.

Intergroup Conflicts

We have seen that in countries that do not have a homogenous population, rapid population growth creates or aggravates political and economic conflicts between racial, cultural, religious, and linguistic groups. The problems of ameliorating these conflicts have not been solved, and they represent a most serious threat to the existence of many states. In some cases, far-reaching measures such as mass migration or fragmentation of states into autonomous or semi-autonomous smaller units may be the only feasible policy options. But governments can do much by a more evenhanded treatment of different groups, providing not only equal but increased educational and employment opportunities and services for all, and by the political and legal devices that protect minorities without jeopardizing the basic interests of the majority.

Through better education and increased opportunities for social mobility, minority groups will learn that population quality is more important than numbers, and that improving quality is largely incompatible with rapidly increasing numbers. Experience shows that, over time, this will lead to lower birth rates and population growth and hence to a reduction in the levels of conflict.

Unemployment and Underemployment

The existence of large and rapidly growing supplies of cheap labor in many less developed countries tends to hold back the adoption of capital-intensive, labor-saving technology in industry, and thereby slows down increases in productivity and in standards of living.

Policies and programs to reduce the growth of the labor force by fertility control can have little effect during the next 15 years, because the young people who will be entering the labor force and seeking employment during that period are already born. For the near future, emphasis needs to be placed on (a) retaining as many workers as possible in agriculture by government policies that favor hand labor and those kinds of mechanization, such as tube wells, small tillers, and grain dryers, that raise the demand for labor by fostering multiple-cropping; (b) service occupations; and (c) relatively small-scale consumer-goods industries that in the aggregate can employ large numbers of workers. At the same time, efforts to increase productivity of these and other workers should be accelerated as rapidly as available resources allow, because only in this way can standards of living be raised. The productivity of labor in many less developed countries is now so low that industries based on it often cannot compete with similar industries in the advanced countries, even when wages are held at a subsistence level.

POPULATION-INFLUENCING POLICIES TO REDUCE POPULATION GROWTH*

Control of population growth is one of the instruments available to governments to accomplish other objectives: economic growth and social development of the nation; improvement of the health and welfare of the people, both the living generation and generations to come; and conservation and improvement of the environment, both the natural environment and that created by man.

Progress in economic growth is usually stated in terms of annual rates of increase in the production of goods and services—the gross national product, or GNP—in the productivity of labor and capital, and in production or income per capita—the gross national product or the national income divided by the number of people in the nation. Growth in per capita income, in turn, can be thought of as an index, or surrogate, for rising levels of consumption of food and other goods and services, and improvements from year to year in education, communications, transportation, technology, housing, and other aspects of social development. Equally important as growth in per capita income is a narrowing of the gap between the rich and the poor, a reduction of poverty in absolute terms, and a greater perception, by the people, of equity in income distribution.

There are other kinds of policies that can be useful in attaining these objectives. Because all policies require the allocation of scarce human and physical resources, governments must necessarily strike a balance between them. In different countries this will depend, among other things, on the level of development, the balance between population and resources, political circumstances, and the administrative capacity of the government.

Some policies that affect population growth can also help to attain other social objectives in other ways. These multi-objective policies are desirable for several reasons, among which is the uncertain effectiveness, up to the present, of government policies designed to bring about demographic change. Profound changes in mortality and fertility have occurred in many countries in recent decades, but the quantitative effects of government policy on these changes are difficult to assess.

Policies to Reduce Mortality

Rapid declines in mortality have occurred in many less developed countries since World War II, resulting in a rapid acceleration of rates of population growth. But further declines can be expected to be modest in these

*See the chapters in Vol. II of this study by Arthur J. Dyck and J. Mayone Stycos.

countries, regardless of government policy, until a markedly higher level of overall economic development has been attained. In other countries in which mortality is still relatively high, governmental policies could bring about a sharp decline in future years. In these countries a drop in death rates may be an essential precondition for a marked reduction in fertility. Fertility and mortality policies are linked. The reduction of fertility is likely also to reduce both infant-child and maternal mortality, and a sufficient reduction of infant and child mortality may be necessary for reduced fertility.

Policies to Reduce Fertility

Time must pass before any development policy can accomplish its objectives. However, different government policies take different amounts of time before their impact is felt.

Time Horizon of Fertility Control Policies. The time spans over which governmental policies to reduce fertility can be expected to have a major influence on population size will generally be longer than the times required for other kinds of development policies (such as investments in natural resources, import substitution, increasing agricultural yields, electrification, and certain kinds of industrialization) to accomplish their objectives. However, the cumulative impact of a policy of fertility reduction, compared with maintenance of present fertility rates, can be very significant over periods of 10 to 20 years. Moreover, the difficulties of undertaking a policy of fertility reduction in a country with a high rate of population growth increase rapidly as time passes. Many more families will need to be involved to obtain a percentage reduction in fertility in future years equal to that which is now attainable with a smaller reproducing population.

In general, policies to reduce fertility have about the same time horizon as other policies designed to improve the quality of human resources, such as education, infant and child health, and welfare services. In drawing up the government budget, setting priorities, allocating administrative manpower, and deciding on alternative uses of resources, fertility policies should be considered in connection with other human resource policies.

Successful policies of fertility reduction will have a delayed impact on some aspects of social and economic development. For example, 5 to 6 years will elapse before a reduction in the number of births will be reflected in a smaller number of children entering primary schools. As we explained earlier, the size of the labor force will not be affected for about 15 years. The rate of family formation and the consequent needs for housing will begin to be lower at about the same time. The full impact on food needs will be delayed until the smaller numbers of children have reached later adolescence (15 to 19 years of age) and their nutritional needs are at a maximum.

On the other hand, a reduction in number of births will affect the need for health and welfare services for both children and mothers. The need for high-quality protein foods to save the lives and ensure the mental and physical development of children, and to protect the health of pregnant and lactating women, will decrease with the birth rate. And pressures for illegal and dangerous abortions will diminish with the successful dissemination of other means of fertility control.

At the micro-level of the family and the village, the effect of a prevented birth will be immediate in terms of smaller family size and a lower dependency burden, with the accompanying economic and health benefits for the welfare of living children and mothers, and the possibility of increased savings and investment by the family for its own future welfare. But the pressures of increased numbers of families on the size of farms, and on young men to leave the village in search of a livelihood, will not diminish until the smaller numbers of children become adults.

Goals of Fertility Control Policies

Developed and less developed countries can be differentiated almost as well by their birth rates, proportions of children, and rates of population growth as by per capita income and other socioeconomic measures. In all developed countries there are less than 20-25 live births per 1,000 people per year, and rates of natural population increase (the difference between birth rates and death rates) are usually lower than 15 per 1,000 per year, which means that the times required for the population to double in size are about 50 years or more. Nearly all less developed countries have birth rates higher than 30 per 1,000, and rates of natural increase higher than 20 per 1,000, with doubling times of less than 35 years.

The principal objective of national fertility control policies in less developed countries is to facilitate economic and social development. It appears reasonable, therefore, to select as the goal of these policies a reduction in fertility and rate of population growth *within the next 2 decades* to a level in the range of that in more developed economies.

We are unable to demonstrate quantitatively the extent to which such a marked reduction in fertility and rate of population growth would influence the rate of development. We are certain only that in all developed societies such a decline occurred during the course of their development. Birth rates in many present developed countries were relatively low even in the early stages of development, and the consequently low proportion of children to adults may have been an important factor in facilitating economic growth.

It is true that the decline in fertility in most of the now developed countries took place over a much longer time span than the 2 decades we have suggested, but the example of Japan, where birth rates decreased by nearly 50 percent from 1948 to 1960, and the rapid rates of decline in Taiwan and South Korea show that under present-day conditions a speedy fall in fertility rates is possible. Today's unprecedented rates of population growth make it urgently desirable. The drop in birth rates in Taiwan and South Korea also indicates that a high level of development is not a necessary condition for fertility decline. A condition that may be equally effective is a rapid rate of economic growth, which allows for social mobility, encourages rising aspirations among the people, and permits the allocation of sufficient resources for fertility control programs and for better communications leading to faster diffusion of information about family planning.

A possible objection is that these fertility ceilings might imply population decline or an undesirably slow rate of population growth in high-mortality nations with low population densities and that it would be unrealistic or unwarranted to expect these nations to endorse such a prospect through deliberate policy. The objection appears to us to have no practical relevance. The overwhelming evidence is that death rates can be brought down greatly and rapidly in low income, high fertility regions throughout the world, by a combination of socioeconomic and public health measures that are economically feasible.

An objection to proposed reductions in population growth rates made by some political leaders is that sheer numbers of people are a prerequisite, or at least an essential element, of political power internationally, especially for small nations. Such power considerations are often claimed to be associated with the achievement of social and economic objectives (such as a sufficiently large market for industrial products) or to override them as policy priorities when the two are in conflict.

There can be no effective rebuttal to those who would knowingly endure the socioeconomic burdens that arise from excessively growing populations in the hope that added numbers will contribute to national power. But the weight of relevant policy considerations seems to us to fall decisively in the opposite direction. First, few, if any, individual goals and certainly no national goals are ever absolute, or independent of the need for weighing priorities. Whatever the prospects for enhanced power or market through added numbers may be, the hoped for benefits must be judged in full awareness of the political, social, and economic costs of too rapid population growth. Second, modernity, not population size or growth, is the strategic determinant of a nation's political and economic status internationally.

A third objection, coming from almost the opposite end of the opinion spectrum is that any fertility target implying a positive rate of population growth is a false or deceptive policy prescription. A correct policy, according to proponents of this view, would aim at zero growth rates everywhere, the more so in the less developed nations since these have a much longer way to go from present vital rate levels and suffer much more severely the adverse consequences of excessive population increase (and often of population size) than do the high income, low fertility nations. Our reply to these claims would not be that they need be refuted but that they are essentially irrelevant for policy purposes.

Associated Goals of Family Planning Programs. Governmental family planning programs may have other goals than reducing population growth by lowering birth rates, though this is a prime objective in many less developed countries, particularly in Asia. These other objectives include

1. increasing the ability and freedom of married couples (particularly poor or ignorant ones who do not have access to private medical care) to determine the number and spacing of their children;
2. reducing the number of illegal (and therefore often hazardous or even fatal) abortions by enabling women who do not want to bear a child to substitute safe contraceptive methods for abortion;
3. improving the health of mothers by helping them avoid too many or too closely spaced pregnancies;
4. reducing the number of illegitimate births;
5. protecting the health and welfare of children by persuading and helping parents to limit the size of their families and to lengthen the interval between births; and
6. helping to alleviate poverty by reducing the economic burden on parents created by large numbers of children.

Criteria for Fertility Control Policies

Before adopting a particular policy to reduce fertility, governmental leaders need to ask themselves several kinds of questions, including whether the policy is politically acceptable to most people, how effective it will be, and whether it is economically and administratively feasible. But the most fundamental questions are ethical: Will the policy enhance the freedom of human beings as individuals, and will it advance justice for all human beings as members of society? These two ethical ideals of individual freedom and distributive justice often are, or seem to be, more or less incompatible. The task of lawgivers throughout history has been to strike a workable balance between them. In establishing a population policy, this reconciliation will be best made if the policy proceeds from the following criteria:*

1. allows for freedom and diversity;
2. where possible, fosters other goals worth supporting for their own sake;
3. does not place unnecessary burdens on innocent people, particularly on children;

*Bernard Berelson, "Beyond Family Planning," *Studies in Family Planning*, 38, February 1969. pp. 1–16.

4. is helpful to deprived and disadvantaged people;
5. is comprehensible to those who are directly affected;
6. shows respect for moral values held by people concerning children and the family; and
7. has as its objective not only economic growth but reductions in poverty, increases in welfare, and conservation of the environment.

Proposed fertility-reduction policies and alternative lines of action need to be examined in the light of these considerations. The problems in any particular case are complex because they require giving different weights to these seven factors and possibly to others as well.

Free Access to Materials, Information, and Services for Fertility Control. Clearly, family planning programs, designed to give full freedom to individual couples to determine the number of their children and the spacing between births, meet several of these criteria. They enhance the freedom of human beings as individuals and, indeed, give this freedom a new dimension, particularly if wives participate equally with husbands in making the decisions. Repeal of laws restricting abortion and free availability of medically safe abortions would further enhance the freedom of individual women and of married couples, and should be considered in those countries that have sufficient medical manpower and hospital facilities and in which public attitudes permit. New approaches to safe induced abortion need to be found in order to lessen the need for medical manpower and hospital facilities.

It is today possible for a full range of acceptable, easily used, and effective means of preventing births to be provided by governments to all persons of reproductive age, if necessary at nominal or no cost. Information on all these means of preventing births, on the economic, social, and health benefits of small family size, and on the cumulative nature of the burdens caused by large families can also be widely disseminated. Steps and actions can be taken to foster broad social legitimization and support of birth control, including, when circumstances permit, medically safe abortions.

Other Policies and Programs

In general, the benefits and costs for society as a whole—that is for all families and individuals in the society—of a child added in one family will be different from those for the parents. These differences* justify social intervention to influence the fertility behavior of the parents. (Another justification for such intervention is that many families need help to recognize and serve their own interests.)

Many specialists are convinced that governmental population policies to limit fertility must go beyond furnishing contraceptive materials, services, and information to individual couples. If these couples, given full freedom of

*Called "externalities" by economists.

choice, on the average decide to have so many children that birth rates and rates of population growth remain high, then the economic and social development of the nation as a whole may be impeded and coming generations of human beings may be handicapped by their very numbers.

The freedom of husbands and wives to make reproductive decisions must, therefore, be tempered by concern for the rights and interests of others. The first and most obvious interest to be protected is that of the children already born within the family. The birth of additional children may affect them adversely in a number of ways, as we have seen. Next come all other members of the society whose economic welfare and social well-being are lessened by rapid population growth, and the younger and subsequent generations, whose opportunities will be diminished by the economic stagnation and loss of amenities caused by this growth. Finally, the interests of other nations and societies must be taken into account, because all nations ultimately make demands on the same pool of resources.

Governments have an obligation to protect the interests of all these groups against excessive reproduction by individual parents. One of the most difficult of population questions relates to designing and justifying governmental policies and procedures to accomplish this end.

Numerous policies have been suggested, some of which are discussed in the sections that follow.

Creation of a Small Family Norm. One policy that would appear to present a minimum restriction on individual freedom and to be well within the generally accepted practices of governments is to encourage private tastes, preferences, expectations, and attitudes toward a small family norm. Educational efforts for this purpose at the community level involve training of local leaders to explain the need for reducing fertility to other members of their communities, group discussions led by family planning workers, and personal persuasion of individuals by these workers. In addition to community-level programs, campaigns of public education and communication through television, radio, the press, outdoor advertising, and other media have also been undertaken. Such community and public efforts are accepted as legitimate components of population programs by many of the less developed countries.

Research on Fertility Control. A policy of generous support of research to improve the acceptability and effectiveness of means of contraception and contragestation (prevention of implantation or development of the fertilized ovum), to achieve reversible sterilization, to find ways of determining the sex of the embryo at about the time of conception, and on social means of achieving fertility decline can be thoroughly justified on both ethical and practical grounds.

Like applied research in agriculture, research in human reproductive biology and psychology should be supported by governments, as should research on other aspects of reproductive behavior. The governments of the developed countries can make very important fundamental contributions to knowledge in this field, but cooperation between developed and less developed countries, and support by the United Nations, its specialized agencies, and other international organizations are needed to accelerate applied research and application, especially social and psychological research and development and testing of new contraceptive methods.

Welfare Policies Leading to Reduced Fertility. The decline in fertility in the Soviet Union, Europe, and North America that took place during the 19th and 20th centuries, and more recent declines in Japan and in some less developed countries, including Taiwan, South Korea, and Costa Rica, strongly indicate that married couples will limit the size of their families if they believe it is in their interest to do so and if means for controlling their own fertility are available to them. The parents' perception of their interest and their corresponding actions depend in part on social traditions and intuitive behavior patterns, as well as on conscious rationality.

Children provide both economic and psychic or social benefits to their parents and to other children in the family. During childhood and youth, they may contribute to family income by working with the family on a farm or in the production of handmade goods, or in a job outside the home. Those children who survive their parents can contribute to their parents' security in old age. Moreover, aside from these economic gains, it is part of our inheritance as human beings that most people like children and want to have some of their own. The psychic rewards of a family life enriched by children are reinforced by social norms, particularly in traditional societies with their extended or clan families and the many benefits conferred by kinship. In addition, the psychic and social costs of preventing births in a society without a high level of contraceptive technology are extraordinarily large, because they almost inevitably involve multiple induced abortions, late marriage, separation of the marriage partners over long periods, or some unsatisfactory modification of sexual relationships.

Children also produce costs, including the money costs of pregnancy and delivery, of feeding, clothing, housing, medical care, and education; the "opportunity cost" of the time and effort spent by parents to bring up their children (the magnitude of this cost depends upon the opportunities that exist for the parents to gain desired goals from other uses of the same time and effort); and the deprivation and health consequences to the mother and her children resulting from an additional child.

Both benefits and costs, as perceived by the parents, will vary with the number and sex of living children in the family. Probably most of the perceived benefits from an added child are highest when the number of children in the family is small. The incremental perceived benefits become less as the number of children increases. Some of the incremental costs of an added child also diminish as the number of children in the family increases, but others, such as the effects on physical and mental health and development, tend to become larger. In those countries, including most of Asia, in which there is a strong preference for sons, the perceived benefits from gaining at least one or two sons will often lead families to risk assuming the costs of several daughters.

Changes in the conditions or way of life that reduce the benefits and increase the costs to the parents of having children, and/or make it easier not to have children, will tend to reduce fertility. Among these variable factors are

1. family income;
2. level of economic, social, and educational development of the society;
3. agricultural versus urban occupation and habitation;
4. possibility and desire for social and economic mobility;
5. availability of arable land and agricultural technology;
6. child labor and compulsory education laws;
7. availability of social security or old-age insurance;
8. employment opportunities for women;
9. status and decision-making ability of women in the society;
10. life expectancy of a newborn child, particulary the probability of survival during infancy and childhood; and
11. availability, effectiveness, and acceptability of means for preventing a birth.

Changes in the first five of these factors are affected by all government policies aimed at economic growth and social development, and are largely determined by the rates of economic growth. But several specific governmental policies and programs which have improvement in welfare as a primary objective will also lower the benefits and increase the costs of having children and are therefore also policies for limiting fertility. These policies are socially beneficial as an integral part of modernization and can be so evaluated quite apart from any effects they may have on fertility. On the other hand, although they are statistically correlated with relatively low or declining fertility, the causal relations are not entirely clear. The quantitative magnitude of the impact on fertility and the time required for this impact are uncertain. Among these multi-objective welfare policies are the following:

Laws prohibiting child labor. The parents lose the benefits of their children's earnings, and their costs are increased because they must support their children rather than letting them pay their own way.

Compulsory education and provision of educational facilities. Children in school have greater material needs; they are less beneficial to their parents because they cannot work when they are in school; and often the parents must pay part or all of the cost of education. Education also has a long-range effect. Educated people, especially educated women, have fewer children than those who are not educated, probably because they perceive their interests differently.

Social security, old-age insurance, and pensions. If old people are supported by the state or through insurance or pension schemes, parents do not have to anticipate depending on their children for income in their old age. The economic incentive for having children is markedly lessened.

Employment opportunities for women. If employment outside the home is available to women, the opportunity costs of having children are increased. A woman who must stay home to take care of her children must forego the income she could earn outside the home. Educational and employment opportunities for young women give them an alternative to early marriage and childbearing, and the age of marriage will tend to rise, with a corresponding lowering of fertility rates. This is clearly occurring in certain districts of the state of Punjab in northwestern India, where the average age of marriage of women has risen steadily from about 17 years in 1956 to over 20 years in 1969, as education and job opportunities for young women in teaching, nursing, and other occupations have opened up. In general, however, an expansion of employment opportunities for women is difficult in less developed countries where unemployment and underemployment are already widespread and the size of the labor force is rising more rapidly than the demand for labor.

Improvement in the status of women. Improving the legal status of women through property, divorce, and inheritance laws, giving women the right to vote and facilitating their exercise of voting rights, and secularization of the marriage contract all tend to give women both a greater share in decision-making about the size of their families, and alternative purposes and opportunities to childbearing, thereby reducing the benefits of having children. By widening their horizons and their circle of communication, women are enabled to obtain better information on means of limiting their own fertility and the reasons for doing so.

Improvement in maternal health. Closely related to improvements in the social status of women are health services aimed at reducing maternal mortality and morbidity. These are both markedly affected by the number and spacing of births experienced by the mother. Policies aimed at improving maternal health should therefore include provision of information and materials for reducing fertility.

Reduction of infant and child mortality. High infant and child mortalities are characteristic of nearly all less developed countries. Considerable reduction is possible through improvements in nutrition, innoculations against infectious disease, and other public health measures. When average infant and child mortalities are high, the uncertainty faced by individual parents concerning the number of their children who are likely to survive is also high. Parents may compensate for this uncertainty by accepting the cost of having "extra" children. Policies and programs aimed at reducing infant and child mortality considerably below present levels, therefore, may be an essential underpinning of governmental programs for fertility control.

Several fiscal and other government policies may also have a direct effect on the costs and benefits of having an additional child. Some of these policies are listed here with a tentative evaluation:

Village financing of education, health, and welfare services. In many less developed countries, the governments are unable to raise sufficient taxes to pay for the expansion of education required to raise enrollment ratios and to keep up with the rapid increase in numbers of children. At the same time, the demand for education among rural people has greatly increased. To meet this demand, it may be necessary to pass part of the responsibility for paying for education to the village level of government. Besides making more education possible, this policy would have the further effect that the villagers would become sharply aware of the costs of having large numbers of children, and would more clearly perceive their interest in lower fertility rates. The same procedure may be necessary and desirable, though to a lesser extent, for public health and welfare services.

Lowering the availability of housing. At least in some countries, the availability of housing appears to affect family formation and the fertility behavior of individual couples in the urban environment. At the same time, housing construction competes for scarce material and skilled labor with other industries needed for economic and social development. In these circumstances, governmental allocation of resources away from housing and toward increasing the means of production in other industries may help reduce fertility. The same result might be obtained by placing occupancy ceilings on housing, that is, limiting the number of people permitted to occupy a given amount of living space.

Military and national service. For national defense and other reasons, many nations require a large proportion of young men to serve in the armed forces. It has been observed that this tends to reduce fertility, at least in part by widening the horizons and the education of the draftees. Compulsory or voluntary national service that fully utilizes the energies and abilities of young women as well as young men could furnish an attractive alternative to marriage and would thus help to postpone the average age of marriage and childbearing—thereby leading to a significant lowering of fertility rates.

Tax and welfare disincentives. Various tax and welfare disincentives have been suggested, for example: abolition of income tax deductions for more than two or three children, an added tax for more than three children; or withdrawal of maternity benefits and family allowances for all but two or three children. These all need careful consideration on ethical grounds: unless a tax were strongly graduated by income, the rich would be affected only slightly, but the poor would be seriously hurt, and the main impact would be on innocent people, namely on the children of large families among the poor, who, as we have seen, are already deprived.

Material incentives for fertility control. Some economists have calculated that nations with a surplus of unskilled labor will save a substantial sum for each birth prevented. From these calculations have sprung a number of plans to share this savings with couples who refrain from bearing additional children. In other words, some kind of payment in money, goods, services, or deferred income would be given to couples in which the wife does not become pregnant.

Under one plan, a married woman under 40 with at least one child would be paid 25¢ a month for the first 4 months she is enrolled in the plan, 50¢ a month for the second 4 months, with payments rising to $10 per year as long as she remains nonpregnant and under 40. Women enrolled in the plan would not only get quarterly payments but also be provided with comprehensive medical services. Under another plan, developed at Ghandigram in India, rewards for nonpregnancy would take the form of community improvements rather than payments to individuals. Under still another plan, couples with, say, three children or fewer at the end of their childbearing period would be entitled to an old-age pension. A fourth plan would provide an educational bond for parents with fewer than a designated number of children.

So far, none of these schemes has been tried even on a pilot basis. Officials of a number of governments have expressed interest in such experiments; others regard them as seriously questionable on ethical grounds. Plans proposed so far seem expensive and difficult to administer; and, until a number of large-scale pilot projects have been attempted to determine their feasibility and acceptability, whether they will induce a significant change in behavior cannot be determined.

The ethical implication of any proposal must also be carefully considered from the point of view of human dignity and distributive justice. Pensions in their old age to parents who have had less than a certain number of children would appear to create little injustice and in the long run might be more than justified by the benefits for all individuals in the society.

Involuntary fertility control. Various schemes for involuntary fertility control have been suggested, including "putting something in the water" that would lower the average fertility of the population, compulsory sterilization of parents after they have acquired more than three or four living children, or compulsory sterilization for all people, which would be reversible only by obtaining a license from the government to have a child. Aside from their political inviability or technical impossibility at the present time, these proposals represent gross violations of individual freedom and would appear to be justifiable on the grounds of distributive justice only after all other methods of limiting population growth have failed.

International sanctions. International pressures on governments of less developed countries to expand and intensify their population control programs, backed up by such sanctions as the denial of food aid to nonconforming countries, have been suggested. Under present circumstances, such a policy would be highly counterproductive from a practical point of view, but it is equally open to condemnation on ethical grounds, because it would violate the principle of distributive justice by penalizing the children of the poorest classes in the poor countries, who are most vulnerable to malnutrition and starvation.

Free education for only two or three children in each family. In a country in which the resources are inadequate to educate all children, it would appear reasonable to place the burden of being not educated in such a way as to encourage parental responsibility, provided all couples had equal and adequate access to means of fertility control. The difficulty here is the practical one—the educational system in most less developed countries could not be so finely adjusted.

POLICY FORMATION AND MANAGEMENT

Population policies are a new and untested area for politicians and administrators, who have neither tradition nor public consensus to guide them. Moreover, because of the long-term quality of population policies, the governments of less developed countries, which are commonly pressed almost beyond their capability by urgent day-to-day problems that may threaten the very stability of regimes, have tended to put population problems and policies to deal with them into the limbo of things to be done when time permits. Most of the economists and planners who advise government leaders have had neither the statistical data nor the analytical tools to be able to fit population questions into their structure of analysis and planning.

The Special Character of Population Policies

These and other difficulties give a special character to the formation of population policies. To create a public consensus, they should be initiated by programs of public education and debate. Because population changes are fundamental to all aspects of the peoples' welfare, leadership needs to be taken at the highest political and government level. To serve national development goals, policies must be based on adequate demographic and economic data. Economic and other advisers need to learn new ways of thinking and new tools of analysis, illuminated by all the knowledge and understanding available in the field. Because population policies must be highly innovative, there is much room for experimentation, and because of their long-term character, experimentation is feasible. But if this experimentation is to be useful, a great deal of attention needs to be paid to realistic evaluation of the results of policies and programs.

Policy Coordination

It is tempting to suggest that population policies are so important, fundamental, and far-reaching that they should be the province of a special ministry of population at the cabinet level within national governments. But the essence of population problems is their pervasive character. Population-responsive policies to deal with the effects of rapid population growth must be part of the responsibility of the ministries that deal with education, health, agriculture, urbanization, transportation, labor, housing, welfare, and even finance and defense. All these ministries need a sophisticated understanding of the ways in which population changes affect their areas of concern.

Similarly, government actions to reduce fertility can be expected to be most successful only if several kinds of population-influencing policies in education, health services, public law, food and nutrition, biological and social research, and social security are brought to bear simultaneously. This calls for coordinated planning and action by many different arms of government. The seat of coordination should be in the jurisdictionally neutral but administratively powerful unit of government that sets priorities in the light of politically established goals. In some countries this will be the planning commission; in others, the executive office of the president or prime minister; in others, a presidential council or commission. The burden of the coordinating task is to ensure that executive agencies with different primary missions manage their affairs through multi-objective population-influencing policies of the kind we have described so as to maximize their contribution to the national goal of fertility reduction.

Administration and Personnel for Population-Influencing Policies

This "systems approach" to population policy requires extensive training of managers, recasting of budgets, development of an international network for exchanging information and ideas, creation of professional standards and career opportunities for population planners and administrators, and organization and funding of many different kinds of research.

As in all fields of government action, population-influencing policies call for the allocation of scarce resources and the setting of priorities. The scarcest resources in most less developed countries are competent administrators, particularly at the lower levels and the front lines of action. Immediate priority is likely to be given to policies and programs that can be combined with other ongoing activities and do not call for the creation of new administrative services: for example, provision of family planning services through existing public health clinics. But policies to control fertility are so important, and so specialized, that in the long run it will be necessary to train, equip, and set in place new administrative cadres.

In part because experienced, specialized personnel for fertility control programs are very scarce but largely because physicians have long thought of birth, like illness and death, as their province, and the public has agreed with them, physicians and other medically trained personnel should be given education and training in population problems as well as methods of fertility control. Their enthusiastic concurrence in fertility control programs is essential in the early stages.

Public information and education are also basic elements of population-influencing policies, whether the concern is for fertility, mortality, or migration. Education and motivation of parents to realize their options, rights, and duties to their own family and to the community must be an integral part of fertility control programs. Specialists in adult and health education and in public communications through newspapers, radio, television, voluntary associations, community leaders, and other means are needed to develop, carry out, and evaluate these tasks.

Multilateral and Bilateral Assistance

Governments can learn from each other's experience in this new field, and they can be stimulated to action by confrontation with effective policies of other countries. The United Nations and its specialized agencies, especially the World Health Organization and UNESCO, can be immensely helpful in this process of intergovernmental learning.

Developed countries can play a major role through bilateral technical assistance in helping to carry out population policies that a developing country would like to establish but which call for greater material, technical, and human resources than are available in the country.

Role of Nongovernmental Organizations

Private agencies dealing with health, family planning, migration, and urbanization problems should be encouraged to continue even after government enters these fields. The private agencies should be looked to for innovation, experiment, and approaches not feasible for governments, rather than for duplication of government services.

Stages of Implementation for Fertility Control Policies

Just as other government policies and programs should be subject to annual review and modification in the light of changing conditions, fertility control policies also need to be kept under scrutiny and frequently modified. In most less developed countries, the first stages of policy will depend on a very considerable improvement in census and vital statistics and their analysis. Public education and debate should be encouraged as soon as possible. Trial programs should be initiated and carefully evaluated. A nationwide organization must be developed, which will function differently in cities than in rural areas. Accurate record-keeping is important, but it should not be pushed too hard at first, nor should quotas and other high-pressure devices be used until a satisfactory methodology has been developed and success seems assured. The program must not move very much faster than the people whom it serves. Their attitudes, values, prejudices, and lack of information must be treated with respect and compassion.

Fertility control policies can be effective only if they change the reproductive behavior of many individual couples. To a large extent in the less developed countries this calls for the efforts of thousands of well-trained, knowledgeable, front-line workers in continuing personal contact with individual men and women in tens of thousands of villages and towns. The problems are somewhat like those of agricultural extension services in changing the agricultural practices of small, independent farmers, and quite different from those of malaria control or mass innoculation programs, which require a minimum of personal contacts. Much of the work is pedestrian, involving meticulous attention to detail and the expeditious solving of day-to-day problems as they arise. Yet the reduction of birth rates in Taiwan and South Korea during the last few years is in considerable part the result of such patient, careful efforts by people at all levels in family planning organizations.

V

Recommendations

This study of the consequences of rapid population growth and their policy implications has led to the policy recommendations that follow. Having offered a number of options in the preceding sections, we now select those we think are the most viable for the near future to help societies cope with and influence population trends.

We are deeply conscious that the issues and actions associated with population questions are of enormous importance in the lives of individual men and women. For this reason we base our first recommendation on the ethical premise that freedom and knowledge should be extended so that people can act in their own best interest—both individually and collectively. It seems quite contrary to society's highest aspirations for men to assume, as some do, that their salvation can be accomplished only through coercion.

Recommendation One: Freedom To Determine Family Size

We urge that governments extend to women and men the freedom and means to determine the number of children in each family and the knowledge which will help them exercise responsible parenthood.

1. A full range of acceptable, easily used, and effective means of preventing births ought to be made accessible by governments to all persons of reproductive age; if necessary, at nominal or no cost.

2. Wide dissemination of full information on all the means of preventing births, on the economic, social, and health benefits of small family size, and on the cumulative nature of the burdens caused by large families should be given high priority both by governments and private institutions.

Information and advice about family planning must be factual and based as far as possible on the special conditions in each country. Very few countries come even close to fulfilling these ideals, not even the developed countries, which can most easily afford their costs. Real freedom of choice of family size with access to the best modern technology of fertility control is completely beyond the reach of well over half a billion families on the earth today.

3. Legal and social barriers to fertility control should be promptly removed and broad social acceptance and support of fertility control should be fostered, including, where health services permit, medically safe abortions and sterilization.

RECOMMENDATION TWO: NATIONAL POPULATION-INFLUENCING POLICIES

To serve national objectives of economic development, public health and welfare, and environmental conservation, we recommend that all nations establish policies to influence the rate of growth of their populations and to adopt politically and ethically acceptable measures toward this end that are within their administrative and economic capability. For most nations of the world the major goal of population-influencing policies should be a reduction in fertility.

Responsible population-influencing policies require adequate demographic data and analysis and will always take into account the attitudes and felt needs of the people. They can be formulated best in the light of economic and political analysis of the complex interrelationships between population growth and economic and social development and with full understanding of the benefits to individual families of a small number of children in each family.

1. The highest level of government is the natural locus for leadership in the formulation of population-influencing policies and the coordination of policy-implementing programs.

Many departments of government, including those concerned with education, health and welfare, public laws, food and nutrition, biological and social research, housing, social security, and national service, should be involved in planning and carrying out welfare and other policies that have fertility reduction as one objective. These policies can best be coordinated and resources allocated for their implementation by the planning or budgeting agencies of governments if they are to make a maximum contribution to the national goals of fertility reduction.

2. Public policies and programs pertaining to human fertility require review at frequent intervals to facilitate modification in the light of changing conditions.

There is much room for experimentation because such programs are highly innovative, but the experimentation will be most useful only if the results are realistically evaluated. If they are successful, the programs will pass through a series of stages. At all stages, the attitudes, values, and level of information of the people being served should influence the program planners.

The effects of population shifts, urbanization, mortality reduction programs, and other population-influencing factors must be carefully weighed as conditions change, because age and sex distribution patterns, as well as population density, create a continuously changing matrix for policy.

RECOMMENDATION THREE: SHORT-TERM GROWTH RATE, DEATH RATE, AND BIRTH RATE GOALS.

First: We urge that countries in which rapid population growth is now occurring seek to reduce their rates of natural increase to less than 15 per 1,000 per year over the next 2 decades. Relatively low-fertility countries that are already growing more slowly than this should seek to approach more closely a stationary population level over the next 20 years.

Second: We urge that in high-mortality countries, modernization policies sufficient to accomplish a reduction in fertility be accompanied by policies of equivalent priority in order to reduce death rates to less than 10-15 per 1,000 per year.

Third: We urge that high-fertility countries set as a goal of population policy the reduction of birth rates within the next 2 decades to less than 25-30 live births per 1,000 people per year.

What constitutes a rational fertility level will obviously vary with circumstances, but we urge that significant limits can and should be identified. Thus it seems to us that there are clear disadvantages of a national birth rate above 30 live births per 1,000 people per year. The weight of evidence and rational presumption concerning socioeconomic consequences strongly favors a birth rate of 25 or less over one of 35 or higher. It is unquestionably desirable for the welfare of children and mothers to reduce the number of children ever born in the average family to a much lower level than the range of six or more that now exists in many countries.

Within the proposed limits on birth rates, individual societies and nations would find ample room for specific policies of fertility reduction that meet their criteria of cultural self-determination and socioeconomic prudence.

As death rates are brought below 10-15 per 1,000 in present high-fertility, high-mortality countries, birth rates should be correspondingly reduced. For present low-fertility countries, the recommendation implies an effort to approach a "replacement level" of fertility.

The magnitude of the policy challenge underlying the attainment of the above proposed limits on fertility is extraordinary. For the large majority of the world's population and for nearly all less developed nations, a drop in the birth rate below 25-30 per 1,000 per year would represent a historic break with the past and would be spectacular if accomplished within 1 or 2 decades. Demographically, the fertility targets being urged here represent a call to revolutionary demographic transition, moderated by a precautionary regard for cultural pluralism, and by a generous allowance for different socio-economic welfare goals in different parts of the world.

Moreover, the central point of the recommendations is that they contemplate the near future—the next 20 years. From a practical point of view, little is gained by proclaiming the virtues of very long-term demographic equilibrium conditions, even if these virtues could be demonstrated uncontestably. Indeed, we see room for harm if such an approach were to usurp the place of considered deliberation by national leaders about needed next steps toward demographic amelioration. A policy approach that proposes an unrealistic goal and threatens disaster if it is not adopted is likely to promote, rather than allay, apathy or opposition.

RECOMMENDATION FOUR: ACCELERATING THE TREND TOWARD THE SMALLER FAMILY

Governmental and private efforts should be expanded to accelerate the trend toward the smaller family and the sense of individual responsibility toward society.

Planned and coordinated factual campaigns of public education and communication through television, radio, the press, outdoor advertising, voluntary associations, community leaders, and personal explanation by family planning workers are means to accomplish this end.

True freedom to determine family size can be realized only if it is, like all other human freedoms, tempered by the concern of the individual for the rights and interests of others. The essence of the matter is to protect both society and the individual. In this instance society needs protection from the undesirable effects of high fertility and the individual needs protection from ignorance, coercion, and inequitable access to the technical resources of society.

RECOMMENDATION FIVE: MULTI-OBJECTIVE POLICIES

We recommend that many of the social policies of governments include among their objectives that of increasing the desirability of small families.

The attitudes of parents toward family size are most likely to change if the social environment, opportunities, and personal relations are altered in ways that help parents perceive their interest differently.

Policies that increase parents' interest in small families, while at the same time serving other desirable goals, include laws prohibiting child labor; compulsory education and provision of educational facilities; social security, old age insurance, and pensions; employment, educational, and career opportunities for women; improvement in the status of women; improvement in maternal health; and reduction of infant and child mortality.

Other policies, related to methods of financing education and welfare services, allocation of resources and occupancy levels for housing, and various types of compulsory or voluntary national service, can likewise be directed toward reducing fertility, as well as toward other objectives.

Population policies should be understandable and widely acceptable to the people. They should help children and the poor and deprived, not place burdens on them. This approach in reducing fertility is particularly relevant for policies involving tax and welfare incentives and disincentives. The alleviation of poverty and greater welfare both for children and adults is the ultimate objective and should be clearly perceived as such by the people.

RECOMMENDATION SIX: POPULATION-RESPONSIVE POLICIES

We urge that policies designed to deal with the effects of population change be established by government departments concerned with education, health, agriculture, urbanization, transportation, labor, housing, welfare, finance, and defense.

Economists and planners who advise these agencies can enhance their effectiveness greatly by seeking greater knowledge and understanding of the ways in which population changes affect their areas of concern and by developing the demographic and economic data and analytical tools needed for this purpose.

The changing effects of age and sex distribution patterns and shifts in population density make population-responsive policies ever vulnerable to short- and long-term demographic changes, many of which can be anticipated by close examination of trends. Policymakers and planners must be alert to these changes as they affect current legislation and administrative practice and as they set the stage for the future.

RECOMMENDATION SEVEN: POPULATION POLICY IN THE INTERNATIONAL CONTEXT

We recommend that developed countries expand their multilateral and bilateral technical assistance to developing countries by providing material, technical, and human resources to help carry out policies and programs aimed at lowering mortality and fertility, improving the conditions of urbanization, and solving other population problems.

It is vital to recognize, however, that population programs and support for fertility limitation cannot be regarded as a substitute for long-term assistance designed to raise people's standards of health, education, consumption, and welfare. A rapid decline in fertility may not be possible without rising levels of education and communication.

Technical assistance can often be effectively provided directly by a developed country to a developing one or by one developing country to another.

The developed countries cannot fail to recognize the long-term nature of many aspects of population problems and their profound relationship to national aspirations in the developing countries. Multilateral and bilateral programs of technical assistance require continuity over many years and should emphasize economic and social development as a primary goal.

By virtue of its leadership in population research and its commitment to the enhancement of the lot of the poor of the world, the United States of America is in a unique position to provide continuing support on a long-term and unequivocal basis to help other countries and international agencies carry out voluntary fertility-limiting programs.

1. The United Nations and its specialized agencies, particularly the U.N. Fund for Population Activities, the World Health Organization, and UNESCO, ought to give high priority to helping their member states learn from one another about population goals and the conduct of fertility-reducing programs.

Information exchange among countries has been one of the most successful activities of the United Nations agencies in other fields, and these agencies are uniquely qualified for this function. Among the promising possibilities is the "confrontation" technique of the Organization for Economic Cooperation and Development.

2. The United Nations Development Program and other U.N. agencies and regional organizations, such as the Pan American Health Organization and the Organization of American States, are urged to greatly strengthen their staffs and procedures to increase the effectiveness of their technical assistance for fertility-reduction programs. Multilateral assistance through intergovernmental agencies will often be more acceptable than bilateral assistance to developing countries; therefore it is important to improve its quality.

3. A United Nations agency (such as the World Bank) should take the lead in preparing a world budget of the needs during the next 2 decades to carry out programs of fertility and mortality reduction in all developing countries.

Such a world budget would be comparable to the *Indicative World Plan for Agricultural Development* prepared by the Food and Agricultural Organization. It is suggested that it include, among other things, provision for research; training; collection and analysis of demographic data; public education and communications; contraceptive materials; services of physicians, paramedical and other personnel; transportation and other expenses; program evaluation; and welfare policies that would reduce the desired numbers of children and are feasible in different countries. It will be important to try to forecast alternative sequences of program development and identify potential sources of funds and modes of financing; particularly the requirements for technical and financial assistance among countries.

4. We applaud the work of foundations, voluntary associations, and other private organizations and urge that they be encouraged in research and action programs for fertility reduction.

The private agencies are a superb source to be looked to for innovation, experimentation, and approaches not feasible for governments, rather than for duplication of government services.

RECOMMENDATION EIGHT: THE NEED FOR RESEARCH

To the student of population problems the need for further research is painfully obvious. Our study on the policy implications of rapid population growth has demonstrated this need to us with extraordinary clarity. It is the habit of scholars to call for more research, but the case for population research appears to us to be compelling for the people of the world. Therefore:

First: We urge that governments, in both developed and developing countries, support research on reproductive physiology and methods of fertility control and on the economic, social, and health factors that determine fertility behavior.

International cooperation in such research can contribute greatly to its effectiveness because the many types of research needed in different cultures, the interdisciplinary character of such research, and the numbers of institutions and people involved require global exchange of information and mutual assistance.

Second: In addition to strengthening ongoing efforts, we propose that a number of international research centers on population problems be established and supported, at least in part, through intergovernmental technical assistance mechanisms.

Third: We urge governments and private agencies to expand university research and teaching on the role of demographic factors in economic and social change.

Problems concerning which more information and understanding are needed include the consequences of population change for economic and social development; urbanization and internal migration; labor policy and industrialization; agriculture and nutrition; health and welfare; education and communications; natural resources and environmental quality; and conflicts among ethnic, linguistic, and other social groups.

These recommendations and our comments are not designed to present a comprehensive solution to the world's population problems; they are simply our selection of the most useful options as of summer 1970. We have, as one result of this study, come to realize that comprehensive closure on most aspects of population is impossible simply because we do not know enough. This is our best estimate of the immediate needs in terms of both prompt action programs for the next few years and the research required to make future policies more effective through an expanded base of knowledge.

Index, Volume I

Abortion, induced: and health services, 56, 58; and population policy, 79, 81, 82, 94
Age, characteristics of, 38-39
Age structure: and health services, 55-56; patterns of, 9-10; political and social implications of, 3, 37-39, 44; and population policy, 95, 97. *See also* Enrollment ratios
Africa, 6, 10-11, 40-41
Aggression, 3, 34-35
Agriculture: and environment, 4, 68; and population policy, 72-76, 90, 97; and rapid population growth, 2, 6, 23-27, 32, 73, 85; technology in, 12, 24-26, 31-32, 43, 72-75; and trade, 21-22. *See also* Food supply; Green Revolution; Labor force
Albania, 8
Asia: agriculture in, 73-75; energy use in, 19-20; population patterns in, 6, 10, 12; urbanization in, 40-41

Balance of payments, 25
Barbados, 8, 14
Birth control. *See* Contraception; Family planning
Birth interval, 55, 60, 61, 63
Birth rates: in developing countries, 8, 10-11, 22-23, 29, 79; history of, 7, 9; policy goals for, 29, 95-96. *See also* Fertility; Population growth

Canada, 8
Capital-intensive technology, 76
Capital investments, 30, 31, 71, 72, 74
Census, 92

Ceylon, 8, 14
Child labor, 39-40, 85, 96
Children: benefits and costs of, 18, 84-86; desired and actual numbers of, 12-14; health and welfare of, 3, 22, 56-57, 81, 83. *See also* Family size
Chile, 8, 14
China, People's Republic of, 6, 14
China, Republic of (Taiwan), 12, 13, 14; fertility declines in, 8, 10-11, 80, 84
Chinese culture, 9
Cities, 19; health levels in, 59-60; population in, 41-42; primary, 45; size and location of, 44-46, 47, 70, 75-76. *See also* Urbanization
Colombia, 14
Communications, 5, 8, 80, 91, 96, 99
Consumer surplus, 26
Consumption, 27, 29, 65, 77, 97
Contraception, 14, 57, 98. *See also* Family planning
Costa Rica, 8, 14

Death rates, 1, 24; goals for, 95-96; rural vs. urban, 59-60; types of, 10-11. *See also* Mortality
Defense, 97
Demographic transition, 7, 9, 37, 95
Density: and developing nations, 12, 13, 24; and health, 58-60; social effects of, 34-36, 66-67. *See also* Urbanization
Dependency ratio, 2, 9, 30, 79; definition of, 38; and education, 48-49
Developed countries: age structure in, 9-10; contrasted with developing countries, 18-20, 21-23, 28-30, 42, 49-50, 67-68, 79; population goals for, 95; population projections for, 6-7, 12

101